UNAMUNO

U N A M U N O

A Philosophy of Tragedy

By José Ferrater Mora

Translated by Philip Silver

GREENWOOD PRESS, PUBLISHERS
WESTPORT, CONNECTICUT

Library of Congress Cataloging in Publication Data

Ferrater Mora, José, 1912–
   Unamuno, a philosophy of tragedy.

   Translation of: Unamuno, bosquejo de una filosofía.
   Reprint. Originally published: Berkeley : University
of California Press, 1962.
   Bibliography: p.
   1. Unamuno, Miguel de, 1864–1936. I. Title.
B4568.U54F43 1981   196'.1   81–20162
ISBN 0-313-23341-1 (lib. bdg.)   AACR2

Translated from *Unamuno: Bosquejo de una filosofia,*
second Spanish edition 1957, Buenos Aires, Editorial
Sudamericana, with extensive revisions by the author.

Reprinted with the permission of University of California
Press.

Reprinted in 1982 by Greenwood Press,
A division of Congressional Information Service, Inc.
88 Post Road West, Westport, Connecticut 06881

Printed in the United States of America

10 9 8 7 6 5 4 3 2 1

Preface to the American Edition

THERE ARE at least three ways of studying the work of an author and, in particular, that of a philosopher: the erudite, the critical, and the interpretive.

Those who employ the erudite approach are, or claim to be, impartial. Their mission is to amass (and, whenever necessary, correct) facts and dates, edit texts, unearth documents, sort out epochs and phases, inventory themes and motifs, trace relationships, discover books read, and track down influences. The work of erudition is, of course, necessary; more than that, it is indispensable. Without it one runs the risk of committing pompous falsifications or pronouncing solemn nonsense. Without an existent apparatus of erudition, the honest study of any author is impossible.

Those who employ the critical approach begin by adopting positions from which they usually strike out at the writer being studied. When these positions are purely external to, or have little to do with, the system of thought that is their target they obtain success as showy as it is useless. One can criticize Plato, Aristotle, Descartes, Hume, and Hegel with considerable success —particularly if one has the good fortune to have been born much later than they. When the positions adopted by the critics are purely internal, their success is equally notable though less spectacular. To achieve their ends they have only to lay bare the internal contradictions of a system and show that the conclusions would have been otherwise if the author had been faithful to his premises.

Neither of these two variations on the critical approach

seems to me acceptable. The first is based upon a falsification; the second, upon pedantry. There is, however, a third variety of the critical approach which is much more respectable. This is the criticism of another system of philosophy using one's own philosophy as a point of reference—if, of course, this latter is fully evolved, mature, and not simply a series of more or less arbitrary opinions. And even then one's own philosophy should in some way be related to the philosophy to be criticized.

Those who employ the interpretive approach begin by sympathizing with the author studied. Yet "sympathizing with the author" does not mean identification with all his opinions or the appropriation of all his feelings. If this were to occur, interpretation would be impossible, and the only result would be repetition or, at best, summary. "Sympathizing with the author" primarily means getting inside his work, bringing his attitudes to light, scrutinizing his suppositions, and, above all, understanding his intentions. All this can be carried out in a style of thought different from that of the author being studied. But one must never give way to the temptation of falsifying the author's thought. The sympathy of which I speak is not, therefore, that of adherence, but of comprehension.

My book does not use the erudite approach. It does not pretend to, for much of this work has already been accomplished. Although much is still to be done in the study of Unamuno's themes and motifs, in the analysis of his modes of expression, in the investigation of his changes and crises, we already possess a sufficient body of carefully edited texts and of studies on specific aspects of Unamuno's work so that any future study of him may now rest upon a solid foundation of erudition. Furthermore, although Unamuno said and wrote many things, all of them can be reduced to a relatively small nucleus of preoccupations that tormented him all his life and make his philosophy, in spite of its apparent diffuseness, a singularly well-mortised whole. Nor is my book critical in either of our first two acceptations of that term. I neither adopt external positions in order to refute Unamuno's ideas, nor try to expose his internal contradictions. I might, I hope, have set out my own philosophy and considered Unamuno's in the light of it, but I suspect that the reader is more interested in Unamuno's thought than in mine.

For these reasons, I have used the interpretive approach. This approach is all the more suitable since Unamuno was one of those philosophers with whom there is the danger of being unjust if he is measured by alien standards—standards that lead one all too readily into making the author think and say what would never have occurred to him. I have decided to measure Unamuno by his own standards, even though, by so doing, I have forsworn certain techniques that are particularly congenial to me. It seemed the reader would arrive at a better understanding of Unamuno's personality and thought if I made an effort to expound and interpret them "Unamunianly." And this book would not be faithful to Unamuno if it did not contain a certain amount of disquietude and tension.

It has often been said that Unamuno was an existentialist thinker, or at least one of the forerunners of existentialist philosophy. To the extent that labels and tags aid in the understanding of an author—and even help to make him more widely known —I see nothing wrong with agreeing to such a description. After all, Unamuno's philosophy is nearer to the existentialist or existential philosophies than to any others. Nevertheless, he cannot be adequately understood by merely affiliating him with a philosophical movement. Unamuno evolved a mode of thought into which various important philosophical movements entered in a conflicting way without this conflict ever being finally resolved. Thus, for example, Unamuno was not simply an irrationalist. But neither was he a rationalist. As I try to prove in this book, both irrationalism and rationalism were equal ingredients of his philosophy. The same might be said of other philosophical movements or trends and, therefore, of existentialism. Yet Unamuno was no less an essentialist than he was an existentialist. How reason and faith, essence and existence, heart and head, and even peace and conflict, harmonized and struggled with each other is primarily what I have undertaken to demonstrate in this book.

J. F. M.

Bryn Mawr College
Bryn Mawr, Pa.

Contents

ONE

Unamuno and His Generation

1 The Generation of 1898

MIGUEL DE UNAMUNO was born in Bilbao, the spiritual and indus-
trial capital of the Spanish Basque country, on September 29,
1864. He spent his childhood and a part of his youth there, and
it left an indelible mark on the whole of his life. Unamuno was
always profoundly aware of his "Basqueness," even throughout
his struggle against the political nationalism prevailing in that
region. Far from believing that being Basque and Spanish at the
same time were incompatible, he often urged that the Basques
become the substance and, as it were, the salt of Spain. By so doing,
he ranged himself with a large group of modern Spanish writers
who, though born in the peripheral provinces of Spain, have done
their best to revive the seemingly lethargic center—Castile.

Unamuno passionately adopted this center, but instead of
quietly surrendering to its charm, he tried desperately to rekindle
its fire. Whereas for Unamuno the Basque land was "the land of
his love," Castile must be called "the land of his pain." The two

regions were constantly at war in Unamuno's heart, or, as he saw it, in an unending embrace.

Since Unamuno was born in 1864, it has long been customary to include him in the Spanish literary Generation of 1898. In fact, he has often been considered one of its leaders, and even its most prominent figure. I shall follow here an already well-established usage, but I shall not attempt to explain Unamuno's personality and work entirely on the basis of a generational scheme. For one thing, there are other factors that must be taken into account—the psychological, social, and political, to mention only a few. For another, there are many points on which a writer and his generation are at cross purposes. I would consider the generational approach useful, then, but with the proviso that some limits be placed upon it.

The existence of the Spanish literary Generation of 1898 raises a few questions, and at least two of them must be answered within the compass of this enquiry. The first concerns the members of the generation; the second, characteristics they reportedly had in common.

Answers to the first of these questions have been legion. Some critics have restricted the Generation of 1898 to a small group of writers whose literary achievements and ideological significance are assured—Unamuno, Antonio Machado (sometimes also his brother, Manuel Machado), Azorín, Pío Baroja, Jacinto Benavente, Ramiro de Maeztu, and Ramón del Valle-Inclán. Others have felt that although this restriction is qualitatively valid, it is not historically so. Azorín and Baroja have convincingly shown that several writers, once famous but now virtually forgotten (Ruiz Contreras, Ciro Bayo, and Silverio Lanza), contributed as much to the literary climate that allows critics to speak of a Generation of 1898 as those writers who have become a standard part of the history of Spanish literature. Vicente Blasco Ibáñez could also be added to those whom Azorín and Pío Baroja have mentioned. In principle there is no reason why a phenomenal literary success should be considered as sufficient reason for excluding an author from even the most sophisticated histories of literature.

As if this disagreement over the number of writers to be properly included in the Generation of 1898 were not enough, the question of whether or not there were subgroups within the generation has often been asked. Some critics maintain, for example, that very definite subgroups—shaped by personal, literary, or political attitudes—persisted for a long time. Other critics counter by saying that there was by no means any feeling of spiritual coördination among the members of the generation as a whole, or of any particular group within it. Connected with the above questions is another: whether, according to strict chronology, it is even legitimate to include Unamuno in a generation whose other important members were several years his junior,—seven years for Valle-Inclán; ten, for Azorín and Baroja; and no less than thirteen, for Antonio Machado. Confronted with this last problem, some critics and historians of Spanish literature have suggested the following solution: to consider Unamuno and Angel Ganivet (his junior by one year) members of a generation or semigeneration immediately preceding that of 1898. This would make Unamuno a member of an influential intellectual dyarchy occupying an intermediate position between the leading representatives of the Generation of 1898, and that other group or, as it has sometimes been considered, generation of writers to which Joaquín Costa, Juan Valera, Francisco Giner de los Ríos, Marcelino Menéndez y Pelayo, and Benito Pérez Galdós belonged.

Answers to the question of common characteristics of the various members of the Generation of 1898 are equally numerous. According to some critics these characteristics were mainly political or, if one prefers, historicopolitical. To these critics the Generation of 1898 was symbolic of the so-called "Disaster" (the loss of the Spanish overseas colonies after the Spanish-American war) and of the desire to meet this political setback in new, or supposedly new, ways by an inner-directing of the entire nation and a rebellion against all the conventional interpretations of its history. Others thought it was a question of purely literary traits. They felt the Generation of 1898 represented one of the great revolutions in the history of Spanish literature. And lastly, others favored traits at once more personal and more general in nature. They spoke of a community of sentiment at first negatively oriented (a dislike of empty rhetoric, of the routinely official Spain, of spiritual narrowness); but gradually this orientation became more positive in intention and in the results achieved. The most positive aspects of this spiritual renewal consisted in a search for authenticity, a rediscovery of the "real country," and a new sensitivity to the beauty of the language. Such a community of sentiment becomes even more clearly defined when contrasted with the intellectual attitudes current in Spain up until this time. It is by no means certain that the members of the Generation of 1898 reacted in the same ways to all the views held by the leading representatives of preceding generations. But since they often considered themselves, for a time at least, as the sole promoters of the spiritual renewal of which I have spoken, it is reasonable to assume that they had at least one view in common: the conviction (soon shaken by Azorín's indefatigable reconstruction of the Spanish literary past) that what they were doing in the field of literature and literary sensibility was something that no one else had done in Spain since the end of the Golden Age.

Our task here is not to comment at length on the above opinions; it will suffice to point out that although all of them contain information of use to us, they also reveal an important shortcoming: their purely schematic character. Their proponents seem to overlook the fact that there is no such thing as an unchanging nucleus of ideas and attitudes in a literary generation.

It would be more exact to surmise that for a time a cluster of ideas, attitudes, aspirations, and desires were condensed into a changing core. As a consequence, the relations between a writer and his generation display a great variety of forms. It is quite possible for a writer to be a member of a given generation while moving constantly in and out of it. It is possible for a writer to do his work in a direction that a generation will later adopt as its own. It is also possible for a writer to become a member of a generation that has almost completed its cycle. Under no circumstances can it be said, then, that a literary generation is a perfectly definable historical entity and that all the literary achievements of its members exactly reflect the same pattern of spiritual ideals and aesthetic norms. The idea of a literary generation is, in short, not one that we can blindly accept, nor is it one that we can completely do without.

If we now apply this more flexible view to the problem of the Spanish literary Generation of 1898, and to the relationship between Unamuno and this generation, we will be able to conclude (1) that no characterization of the traits of the generation will ever be completely satisfactory, and (2) that Unamuno can be said to have been, and not to have been, one of its members. Thus, for example, although Unamuno and Ganivet were several years older than the other writers already mentioned, they were quite close to the cluster of ideas and attitudes usually associated with the Generation of 1898; indeed, they prepared the way for those ideas and attitudes. To be sure, Unamuno's contact with them was intimate, whereas Ganivet's was only peripheral. Because they both championed certain mental attitudes later developed by the other writers, and especially because Unamuno was hailed (according to Azorín) as a highly respected elder master of the group, they cannot be considered apart from the generation that they so decisively molded. On the other hand, with respect to the controversial issues that occupied the most famous Spanish writers of the time

(Europeanism versus Hispanism, renovation versus tradition, activity versus stagnation), Unamuno assumed attitudes on occasion widely at variance with those of the other members of his generation. Therefore, whenever we accept the conventional picture of the Generation of 1898 and of Unamuno as one of its charter members, we do so with a number of reservations. And the more we consider Unamuno's activities *en bloc* instead of limiting ourselves to his early work, the more important these reservations seem likely to become. For example, there is something to be said in favor of the existence of an "intermediate generation" between that of 1868 (Joaquín Costa, Juan Valera, etc.) and that of 1898, and in favor of considering Unamuno, because of his date of birth, as one of its members. But in view of the philosophical character of Unamuno's work, and because a substantial part of it developed contemporaneously with the work of Ortega y Gasset and Eugenio d'Ors—who were born almost twenty years after Unamuno—we may even lump these three together in a special group connected with, but in no way dependent upon, the ideals promoted by the great majority of members of the Generation of 1898. So it seems that Unamuno was right, after all, when he claimed that he was "unclassifiable." All this helps to explain an apparently cryptic statement by the Spanish sociologist and novelist, Francisco Ayala: that Unamuno, far from being a continuation or a simple hiatus of Spanish tradition, was a true "period and new paragraph"—an abrupt end as well as a radical departure.

2   The apprenticeship years

With all the above in mind I will now trace Unamuno's biography —in particular, his intellectual biography. Above all, I will chart some sectors of his public life. Of course, insistence upon the public aspects does not necessarily mean that they alone are pertinent to an understanding of this philosopher's mind. Unamuno's public life was always deeply rooted in the silence of his inner life, so much so that most of the actions of his public existence emerge as eruptions of that deeper inmost silence. It is unfortunate, moreover, that the profound inner life of a thinker is often beyond the critic's grasp. It is even possible that, like any genuinely private life, Unamuno's will forever remain that famous "secret of the heart" which theologians tell us is revealed only in God's presence. Only by examining what is expressed in his writing—his thoughts, his contradictions, his doubts, his outbursts of joy, of anguish, and of anger—will we be able to catch a glimpse of his secret and his silence.

During the years succeeding Unamuno's birth, Spain gave herself up to such frenzied activity that it was difficult to tell whether the acceleration of her traditionally irregular pulse signaled a new vitality or a new decay. They were years of rebellion and crisis—1868, 1869, and 1870. The various upheavals suffered by the country had not yet coalesced into what would later be called the Second Civil War, fought with extreme fanaticism in the north, particularly when the Carlist siege of Bilbao began in December, 1873. By this time Unamuno, fatherless since his sixth year, was nine. The "first significant event" of his life, he often recalled, was "the explosion of a Carlist bomb" (February 21, 1874) on the roof of an adjacent house. The explosion left that characteristic "smell of powder" in the air around which many of Unamuno's ideas and feelings on Spain were to crystallize. From that moment Unamuno was able to recognize the existence of a tension that was to make itself felt again and again during his life. He realized that it was possible for Spaniards to talk about "the others"—the ones belonging to another faction—while acknowledging that these "others" were no less Spanish than themselves. He observed factions waging a cruel war against one another, and it puzzled him that each one of these factions was composed of true Spaniards in spite of the ideas (or, at times, lack of them) for which they tried to dismember and destroy their enemies. We are today inclined to suspect that underlying these struggles was a complex pattern of social and economic problems. But to Unamuno they presented themselves as a series of obsessions. It was the oppressive and at the same time vitalizing nature of these obsessions that Unamuno sensed during the monotonous days at school, and in the childish tussles he describes in his early autobiography, *Memories of Childhood and Youth* (*Recuerdos de niñez y de mocedad*): angry voices blended with sane words; fierce cruelty linked with deep charity, all the confused shreds of the anarchist and absolutist temperament of Spain's immemorial soul.

The basic experience behind his first novel, *Peace in War* (*Paz en la guerra*), was that smell of powder experienced during the siege of Bilbao. Just as the *Iliad* had been the epic of the Trojan wars, Unamuno intended this novel to be an objective epic of Spain's civil struggles during the third quarter of the nineteenth century. But it is not only a historical moment that is narrated in *Peace in War;* it is, according to Unamuno's own confession, "the essence of his people." He does not confine himself to describing a chain of events; he means to develop all the implications of a collective experience. That is why this book remained for a long time the major source of Unamuno's later interpretations of the Spanish soul. It is also the first complete example of his search for peace in the midst of continual war. In fact, for Unamuno the explosion of the bomb in Bilbao was the first of a long series of Spanish explosions that he was to witness; and in the center of the last and most violent of them all—the 1936–1939 Civil War—he was to die.

A year after the explosion, his primary education finished, Unamuno entered the Instituto Vizcaíno of Bilbao. We know little about him during these "high-school" years (1875–1880), but it seems that the one experience that dwarfed all others was the discovery, in his fervid and random reading, of an entirely new world: the world of ideas. He began to love poetry—the poetry of poets and the poetry of philosophers. A detailed examination of the authors read by Unamuno in these years would be most enlightening; here I may only mention that he avidly read Jaime Balmes—one of the promoters of the nineteenth-century neo-scholastic revival, and a writer whom he later attacked; Juan Donoso Cortés—the leading representative of a staunch tradition-alism; Antonio Trueba, and a host of Spanish Romantic poets. I suspect that he spent a long time reading and rereading his own first poems, an activity he might have defended later by claiming that if they were not original (as most probably they were not at this age) from a literary point of view, they might be original from a personal point of view—originality being for him not a question of craftsmanship, but a question of strong feeling and sincere belief.

When the completion of his "high-school" years in 1880 ended his residence in Bilbao, he went on to Madrid for university studies, which occupied him until 1884. There he plunged feverishly into a turmoil of philosophical ideas and religious doubts; and there, like his hero, Pachico, in *Peace in War,* he passed his days "hatching dreams." It appears that Madrid was not much to his liking. Unamuno, the native son of a provincial town, at that time still more rural than urban, was probably ill at ease in a city like Madrid which, while already proud of her meager cosmopolitanism, was a thousand miles from that universality which Unamuno felt to be the exact opposite of cosmopolitanism. Nor was Unamuno as greatly influenced by university life as Spanish students were later to be when, with Ortega y Gasset and others, the universities and particularly the University of Madrid gained influence and prestige. Probably more significant and influential than Unamuno's univer-sity life was his own voracious and diverse reading and his contact with the writings and the personalities of some of the dominant intellectual figures in the Spanish capital. The intellectual personalities then in ascendancy, or long since firmly established, spanned several generations, from those who, like Francisco Pi y Margall—the highly respected left-wing historian and political writer—had been born in 1821, to men like Joaquín Costa—the versatile man of letters—born in 1846. The same time span also included a more compact generation, that is, one of men born about the year 1838. This so-called generation of 1868 included those deans of Republicanism, Emilio Castelar and Nicolás Salmerón, the educators Francisco Giner de los Ríos and the writers Pedro Antonio de Alarcón, José María de Pereda, Juan Valera, and Benito Pérez Galdós. Most of these men shared a desire to rejuvenate Spain, a desire that was as apparent in the skeptical and somewhat snobbish accents of Valera as it was in the trenchant language of Costa. Numerous controversies took place in this connection. The "Krausists" and the "Catholics" opposed each other in the most important of these controversies, each side representing not only different ideological currents and world views, but also, and perhaps above all, different temperaments. Unamuno picked his way among the spiritual peaks of his day, now in sympathy with one, now with another. To be sure, some temperaments attracted him more than others. He chose at that time the liberal, europeanizing group, and sided with the enterprising renovators who, guided by Costa, meant to "lock the Cid's tomb with seven keys." These renovators intended to put a stop to Spain's quixotic antics and to her unchecked "Cidismo." All this was very far from Unamuno's later thoughts on Spain's past, but nevertheless it freed him from the conventional, shallow views held by the extreme "traditionalists." At any rate, this was the intellectual climate of Madrid between 1880 and 1884 which influenced Unamuno more than the university ever could.

After four years of study, of silence, of solitary meditation, "wrapped in one's own thoughts," of debates in student rooms, at the Círculo Vasco-navarro and the Ateneo, of long walks (Unamuno was already, and remained until his death, an indefatigable stroller), he received his doctoral degree and returned to the Basque provinces and an outwardly uneventful life. With his return to Bilbao and his renewed residence in the Basque countryside between 1884 and 1891, past experiences began to arrange themselves meaningfully for him. He earned his living by giving private lessons, found time to read extensively, to participate in discussions at the Sociedad Bilbaína, and to walk for long hours through the streets. He soon became aware of a historical horizon that would serve perfectly as the setting for a narrative. He focused his interest on the Second Carlist War as symbolic of a chronic phase of Spanish life. While he gave lessons, wrote unsigned articles for a Socialist newspaper, and prepared for his professional competitive examinations, he collected an enormous fund of anecdotal information about the war from the lips of survivors and by a continual reëxamination of his own childhood memories. With this information at hand, he tried to reconstruct the climate of the war as faithfully as possible. As I have said, he wanted to write a truly novelistic epic. Outlined as early as 1890, *Peace in War,* at first a short story, was not published in book form until 1897. In order to write the book, which was to become a long novel, Unamuno needed a spiritual and economic tranquility that Bilbao, for all its "charm," could not offer. Unamuno's literary labors needed new soil for their fruition; this was to be Salamanca, in the very heart of Old Castile.

3   The critical years

Unamuno went then to Madrid, and spent several months taking various competitive examinations for a teaching position. After several attempts at various positions, he won a chair of Greek language and literature in Salamanca. Valera and Menéndez y Pelayo, the defenders of two opposing points of view—the "modern" and the "traditional"—were among his examiners. These examinations took place in the spring of 1891, and it was then that Unamuno met Ganivet in whom he recognized a restless spirit akin to his own. Both were deeply involved in a quest for an authentically Spanish system of thought unaffected by external europeanizing influences and untarnished by Spanish "traditionalism." If in Ganivet this concern was disguised beneath a mask of ironic bitterness, in Unamuno, a more positive and more vital person, the concern was readily visible, based as it was upon an agressively polemical nature. Both, however, drew on similar experiences; both were convinced that a Spanish philosophy could be distilled from Spanish life, rather than culled from the books on library shelves; both felt that, as Ganivet had written, "the most important philosophy for any country is one native to it, even though inferior to the able imitations of foreign philosophies."

Later in 1891 Unamuno moved to Salamanca, an event that marked for him the beginning of a new epoch. Salamanca came to mean more than an administrative position to Unamuno. His residence in this quiet city helped him to discover himself, his possibilities, and, in a sense, his limitations. There were few cities that could have provided a more perfect setting for his type of thinking than Salamanca, so heavy with silence and history, its *agora* interlaced by fields, and its immense plains set under high mountains. Here was a city in which to discover immutable truths beneath the transitory anecdotes, the living bedrock of "eternal tradition" beneath the continual upheavals of history. In his lifelong tenure at Salamanca there was, moreover, a decisive period for Unamuno; it came between the publication of *On Purism* (*En torno al casticismo*) in 1895 and *The Life of Don Quixote and Sancho* (*Vida de Don Quijote y Sancho*) in 1905. The zenith of this period was the year 1897. He had experienced a great intellectual crisis in Madrid, but the one in Salamanca was to be more profound, more emotional, more intimate, and more religious. Even assuming that Unamuno's religious crisis had been less profound or less sudden than Antonio Sánchez Barhudo has detailed it, there is little doubt that a profound experience, or series of experiences, gripped Unamuno's soul. At any rate, there is a definite change in tone in his writing before and after 1897. Before 1897, and particularly between 1895 and 1897, we find Unamuno in a pitched battle with "purism" and traditionalism, which he declared to be empty and conventional. Local tradition, he argued, must be discarded in favor of universality. Repetition must give way to renovation; Spain must be prodded from the bog that held it fast. After 1897, however, and especially between 1897 and 1905, we find Unamuno absorbed in a tense and painful attempt at innerdirection. Here the *Three Essays* (*Tres ensayos*) of 1900, with their passionate inquiry into the problem—or rather, mystery—of personality, individual and collective, is a salient landmark. Unamuno's "Inward!" replaces his cry of "Forward!" Don Quixote replaces Don Alonso Quijano; and the stuff of dreams, no longer a stumbling block, becomes the very substance of existence.

It is true that there seems to have been some preparation for these new views during the two or three years preceding the "great crisis." After all, though Unamuno defended—before 1897—the importance of forms and symbols, and the stuff of which, he said at that time, the world was constructed, he also maintained that the former possessed "feelings" and the latter, "life." Therefore, the name, the incarnation of a concept must "repossess itself in the permanent, eternal realm"; forms and symbols were no longer to be considered attributes of an intelligible world, but of a more substantial universe—a sensuous *and* an eternal one. That is why the universality, which Unamuno opposed to cosmopolitanism, belongs to the "eternal tradition" that exists beneath the surface of routine conventions. But his ideas on the same questions became much more trenchant, and in many ways more searching, after 1897. If Unamuno underwrote tradition at this time, it was as something quite unlike that seclusion-within-one's-self practiced and preached by the traditionalists. For Unamuno, "seclusion within one's self" (*encerrarse*) meant a definite "opening inward" (*abrirse hacia sí mismo*). Already in a small way before 1897, but much more after this year, he felt the need to "accumulate continually in order continually to pour forth, to empty one's self," or, as he once described it, "draw in in order to expand" (*concentrarse para irradiar*).

In the light of this process we can understand how Unamuno moved from an eager receptivity to outside forces to a ceaseless pouring out from within, from the apparent "realistic objectivity" and accumulation of detail in *Peace in War* to the "critical subjectivity," the spareness and whimsicality of the novel *Love and Pedagogy* (1902). This is an abrupt change in tone, but we must not forget that it is but a modulation of the same melody that permeated all of Unamuno's work and life.

4   *University and politics*

During these years Unamuno's public life seemed a well-regulated routine of lectures at the university, conversations, discussions, and walks. These occupations were practice for the more resounding activities of the days and weeks he spent in Madrid, where he quickened the pulse of literary and political gatherings in cafés, in the newspaper and literary review offices, and at the Ateneo. Contact with the emotional atmosphere of Madrid soon drew him into politics, but from his first visits to Madrid as a respected writer until his death, his manner of participation in politics was ever characteristically his own. Unamuno never belonged to any one political party; he was too pleased and too proud of being a heretic to all parties—and all regimes. He felt the need continually to disagree, and he saw himself in the role of "spiritual agitator," for at that time he was convinced that what Spain, and Europe, needed most was a quickening of the pulse and a stirring of the soul.

He became still more of a political heretic in 1914, after his dismissal from the post of rector in the University of Salamanca. The government declared that politics and the teaching profession were incompatible. To this pronouncement Unamuno countered by saying that they were, in fact, the same thing; for whereas politics is teaching on a national level, teaching is talking politics on a personal level. And to those who thought that this was only a paradox, he replied that paradoxes could not be dispensed with when it was necessary to jolt an indolent nation awake.

It has often been said that Unamuno was an impassioned

personalist in his philosophy as well as in his politics, and that whereas the first is acceptable, the second is intolerable. This view overlooks two points: first, that it is unfair to expect a complete divorce of thought and action in Unamuno; and second, that his concern with the personal element in politics had its strict counterpart in his philosophy. Both were manifestations of one and the same attitude. At all times this "personalistic" feeling pervaded Unamuno's political life. When he expressed, as he was often to do, antimonarchist sentiments, it was never as an attack on the concept of monarchy and the royal prerogative as such. He attacked one monarchy and one king only, and he felt that this was proof of his predilection for concrete realities. This explains why Unamuno was always considered (and often angrily denounced) as an unstable political element: he was not a Monarchist, but this did not make of him, strictly speaking, a Republican. He was at all times what he wished to be: the dissenting element of all political parties, the troublemaker in all political rallies.

After Unamuno's dismissal as rector of Salamanca, his political activity increased, and he undertook two violent campaigns: one against King Alfonso XIII; the other, against the Central Powers and in defense of the Allied cause in World War I. It is imperative to remember, however, that politics never occupied Unamuno entirely, and that beneath it—often nourishing it—his literary and spiritual life continued as before. Between the publication of *The Life of Don Quixote and Sancho* in 1905 and the publication of his profoundest work, *The Tragic Sense of Life,* in 1913, the channel of his personal inner life broadened and deepened. We have as proof the publication of *Poems* (1907), of *Memories of Childhood and Youth* (1911), of *Rosary of Lyric Sonnets* (*Rosario de Sonetos líricos*) (1911), and of the volume entitled *Through Portugal and Spain* (*Por tierras de Portugal y España*) (1911). This last book is characteristic of his manner of travel and observation, for he appears at once captivated by the circumstantial and seduced by the eternal. These trips through Portugal and Spain thrilled Unamuno to the point of ecstasy, and his myopic perusal of France, Italy, and Switzerland contrasts sharply with the penetration he leveled at his own country and that of his "Portuguese brothers." Baroja wrote that Unamuno saw little or nothing in his European travels because of his fierce intransigence and his intellectual blindness. Baroja's remark is true, but only in part. For Unamuno's blindness was largely fostered by a desire not to allow his observation of foreign lands to distract him from the passionate contemplation of his own. At any rate, although we may complain that Unamuno was not objective enough when he looked north of the Pyrenees, we must thank him for having discovered so much south of that mountain range.

By 1914, Unamuno had become the undisputed mentor of many young Spaniards. This does not mean that he was always listened to with reverence; indeed, he was often violently opposed. But his towering figure made itself felt in the arena of Spanish thought, and there vied for leadership with the other outstanding figures of his time. His chief competitors were Ortega y Gasset, who had been publishing in newspapers since 1902 and had sent his *Meditations on the "Quixote"* (*Meditaciones del Quijote*) to press by 1914; and Eugenio d'Ors, who began publishing his *Commentaries* (*Glosas*) in 1905. The writing of these two differed considerably from Unamuno's both in style and content. Ortega offered a continental manner that was more than a servile imitation of Europe, and d'Ors a twentieth-century viewpoint that was infinitely more appealing than an irrational exaltation of our Age. Because of the order, lucidity, and harmony that they proffered, their work was more acceptable to many than Unamuno's. Small wonder that there were frequent displays of enmity among the three philosophers and their followers. But the enmity gradually subsided as it became apparent that where one was weak another was doubly strong and that, in all fairness, none of the three was

expendable. If some signal issue had been overlooked by Unamuno
it was certain to appear in an essay by Ortega or a commentary
by d'Ors, or vice versa; thus, by supplementing his work with
theirs, they exposed Unamuno's inevitable, yet fruitful, limitations.

5   The exile

This routine of academic lectures, travels and domestic life,
discussions and political sallies, continued until 1924 when
Unamuno burst more loudly than ever upon the public's ear,
acquiring a notoriety that enormously enlarged the number and
variety of his readers. His opposition to Alfonso XIII reached new
extremes as a result of the Primo de Rivera *coup d'état* in 1923.
His audience with the king, interpreted by some as a desertion of
the antimonarchist ranks, merely exemplified, as he pointed out
in a tumultuous meeting at the Ateneo and in the *El Liberal* offices
a few days after, his unswerving fixity of purpose. It had only served
to reinforce an opposition that reached titanic proportions when
the dictatorship of Primo de Rivera was sanctioned by royal decree.
Since the physical annihilation of famous opponents was not yet
customary in European politics, Primo de Rivera's reaction to this
ideological insurrection was at first fumbling and in the end rather
mild. For some time after the advent of Primo de Rivera's dictatorship, Unamuno continued to voice his protests, and after his exile to
Fuerteventura, one of the Canary Islands, they reached an ever
larger public. He came to feel that this exile was the most important
event in the political life of twentieth-century Spain, and he swore
to do his best to destroy his now deadly enemy—a personal
and, therefore, according to one of his paradoxes, a universal one.
     Unamuno's contrariness during his transfer to the place of

exile would provide a book of anecdotes. The anecdotes, unimport-
ant in themselves, are nevertheless a measure of his warlike attitude
toward the dictatorship, and above all toward the dictator. He
continued to write and speak against the king and Primo de Rivera
from Fuerteventura, and when the editor of the French newspaper
Le Quotidien, to which Unamuno had contributed, arranged his
escape from the island, he went to France in voluntary exile, to
continue there his implacable opposition. A pardon arrived, by
coincidence or political calculation, on June 25, 1924, the same day
that Unamuno left for Paris after less than a year of residence in
Fuerteventura. On his arrival in Cherbourg, his private war with
the dictatorship assumed world-wide proportions for the first time;
Max Scheler mentioned it as one event that helped blacken the
spiritual countenance of Europe in the twenties. Unamuno's
antagonism had several motives, but the foremost of these was the
personal—and, again, according to his much-used formula, the
universal—recuperation of Spain. He raised a persistent voice,
speaking and writing in Spain's behalf and in his own.

Given certain inevitable differences, Number 2, rue de la
Pérouse, in Paris, was not unlike the pension where Unamuno lived
during his student days in Madrid. The occupant was a student
of supreme caliber, receiving visits from noted or dull celebrities.
But there was little satisfaction in it all. To Unamuno the Paris
of the twenties seemed to be a curtain that blocked his view of the
Sierra de Gredos, which towered over Salamanca. Neither the
spirited gatherings at La Rotonde—the famous Montparnasse
café recently demolished to provide room for a moving-picture
theatre—nor the interminable walks through streets teeming with
beauty and history lessened the feeling that Paris was an obstacle
in his path. He continued to publish in the European and South
American press, his fight against the dictatorship never wavered,
but his displeasure with the Spanish political situation inhibited
any full cultivation of his religious and poetic spirit for a number

of years. But his true vocation returned when he moved south to Hendaye within sight of the Spanish countryside across the border. No doubt this authentic vocation was more central than his political outbursts and manifestoes, or the *Free Pages* (*Hojas libres*) he published in collaboration with Eduardo Ortega y Gasset and Vicente Blasco Ibáñez. To him his arrival in Hendaye was like the end of an exile. In *The Agony of Christianity* (*La agonía del cristianismo*) (1925) and in *How a Novel Is Made* (*Cómo se hace una novela*) (1927) there were cries of desperation; in Hendaye the desperation mingled with hope, and their union produced the experiences that with the advent of the Republic, were manifested in *Saint Emmanuel the Good, Martyr* (*San Manuel Bueno, mártir*) (1933) and *Brother Juan or The World Is a Stage* (*El hermano Juan o el mundo es teatro*) (1934). The stay in Hendaye was a genuine spiritual resurrection.

6   The return of the Exile

Externally Unamuno's life in Hendaye was much like the one he had led in Paris. There were informal gatherings at the Grand Café, interviews, and many long walks. With the fall of the dictatorship, in 1930, Unamuno was finally at liberty to direct his steps toward Spain, and on the 9th of February he crossed the border and entered Irún. The nation was wild with jubilation now. Beside themselves, the vast majority of the Spaniards cheered the oncoming Republic, but not all with the same purity of intention. As often happens, many lay in ambush, intent upon its quick destruction and the proclamation of any of the politically extreme ideologies that must mean the eventual death of any truly democratic regime. In this period of exaltation and easy optimism, a bloodless revolution seemed possible. But not even the welcoming speeches on his arrival at Irún, the happiness and enthusiasm of the people, nor the whole pages dedicated in all the newspapers to the return of Spain's most famous exile, could make the hero of all their rejoicing forget the two points that had been his trademark: his concern with "eternal Spain" and his fundamentally heterodox approach to each idea and each person. The motto "God, Country, and Law" (*Dios, Patria y Ley*)* which Unamuno uttered, once across the frontier, may have expressed antimonarchist feelings, but it was not yet, as many had expected, an assertion of Republican faith. Even before the Republic was proclaimed on April 14, 1931, Unamuno, who had done more than most to help realize that day, had begun his opposition, as much the political heretic as ever.

The return to Salamanca on February 11, 1930, was quite another matter. His home was there where the silence, which in the final analysis had nourished the best things of his existence, awaited his return. Any biography of Unamuno which presumes to investigate the core of his personality would do well to devote more space to this return to Salamanca than to either his entrance into Irún or the political demonstrations in Madrid in early May, 1930, on the occasion of his arrival in the capital and his famous address there to the Ateneo. In this speech he called the collaborators of the dictatorship to account, coined sharp phrases such as the well-known "Not *up* to the king, but from the king on down," † and struggled to outline the political future. The cheers with which young members of other generations than his acclaimed him, and the homage of the press, gave the impression that Unamuno had become a full-fledged political leader. He seemed drawn along by the rapid, almost feverish succession of events.

* Trans. note: which echoed, unfaithfully, the traditional phrase: "God, Country, and King" (*Dios, Patria y Rey*).

† Trans, note: "No *hasta,* sino *desde* . . ."

But in his heart he remained a poet and a thinker, an indefatigable seeker of the eternal. He raised his voice in Madrid, but only in the silence of Salamanca was he spiritually at home.

7   *The last years*

The proclamation of the Republic one year later found Unamuno unchanged: longing for the eternal and still a victim of the moment. As rector, Unamuno opened the academic year of 1931–1932 at the University of Salamanca in the name of "Her Imperial and Catholic Majesty, Spain," thereby seeming to announce his opposition to the Republic, even if we take "Catholic" to mean here "universal" rather than a definite politico-religious attribute. What he really attacked, however, was the Republic's haggling over trivialities. The Republic was so absorbed with internecine struggles that it had neither the time nor the disposition for an examination of its own conscience. According to Unamuno this was the first, most important challenge of all—the key to all other problems. He felt it was even a key to the solution and management of what today has become the greatest single preoccupation of all governments, regardless of ideology: the national economy. From 1932 until his death, Unamuno's major preoccupations were the misgivings awakened by a growing willfulness in the masses, and the fear of a rapid spiritual and geographical disintegration of Spain. His articles in *El Sol* and *Ahora* became tinged with bitterness because now no one listened to him, or rather, because he thought that just when his work was beginning to bear fruit in the spirit of a new generation, his words fell on deaf ears. But in spite of deep concern and bitterness he did not lose hope. Repeatedly he exercised those same tactics that had served him well against the dictatorship. Times, however, had changed. He was accused by some of "selling out" to the enemy, he was curtly asked by almost all to define his position—the only thing he could not do. He had always felt it his mission to maintain an undefined—which by no means meant an eclectic—position, and to erase the boundaries between himself and his enemies. People who asked Unamuno to clarify his political position forgot that, as he had often said, he counted his own votes and they were never unanimous.

Finally Unamuno's merit was officially recognized. In 1934, at a magnificent celebration in his honor, he was formally retired from his chair and made "Perpetual Rector" of Salamanca. In 1935, he was made an honorary citizen of the Spanish Republic. These festivities marked the close of an animated era that had included his speeches, edged with grave injunctions and filled with incisive attack, before the Constitutional Congress. The tone of his farewell speech as university professor was more subdued. By now Unamuno realized that the agitation he had fostered, and the pain and strife he had decreed, had reached a danger point and needed modulation. At a time when all over Spain there were ominous signs of the impending Civil War and waves of violent disagreement, the renowned sower of fruitful discord began to preach harmony. In the first pages of *The Agony of Christianity* he had written: "My Spain, now mortally wounded, is perhaps destined to die a bloody death on a cross of swords." In *Life of Don Quixote and Sancho* he had written: "Yes, what we need is a civil war." But now Spain was threatened not by a civil war, a mere bloodletting, but by what Unamuno with great foresight had once called an "uncivil war"; one in which, unlike those he had imagined, there would never be peace in the combatants' hearts.

The life remaining to Unamuno, a towering solitary figure, will always be dwarfed by the magnitude of the war that had begun in

July, 1936. On the last day of this same year, Unamuno died amid communiqués of war, as did two of his great European contemporaries, Henri Bergson and Sigmund Freud, three years later.

For a time after his death he was called variously, traitor, weakling, and turncoat. He had hailed the military rebellion, then he had courageously challenged it; the most ardent supporters of the two factions had reasons to speak in anger against him. But those who have taken counsel with the man and his works will realize that he was always true to himself. To be sure, the little we know of his words and deeds during the last six months of his life is both baffling and distressing. But the question is whether it could be otherwise, for everything is baffling and distressing when it comes from the center of a maelstrom of cataclysmic violence. As if destroyed by lightning, Unamuno disappeared in the midst of this historical whirlwind. For a time, his voice was submerged. Some expected that it would remain so forever. They did not realize just how serious Unamuno had been in his intention to make each line he wrote vibrant with the life that was his own.

TWO

The Man of Flesh and Blood –
The Idea of the World – The Idea of God

8 Homo sum

"PHILOSOPHY is the human product of each philosopher, and each philosopher is a man of flesh and blood speaking to other men of flesh and blood." Thus reads the opening sentence of Unamuno's *Tragic Sense of Life*. Never before have the human condition of philosophy and the "earthly" constitution of the philosopher been stated in such radical terms. To be sure, 'human condition' and 'earthly constitution' are hardly expressions that Unamuno would have used himself; he would have shunned both as bloodless abstractions. The individual person, the substance that underlies both philosophy and the philosopher, was what mattered most to Unamuno. He often proclaimed that the individual, concrete human being is the inescapable point of departure for all philosophers worthy of the name.

A "point of departure" as clear and sweeping as Unamuno's implies first the elimination of all idols—particularly the ideological ones. Thus, the first step that Unamuno proposes—especially when writing in a strongly pragmatic vein—is the breaking of and with ideas. Now, Unamuno's pragmatism, unlike the usual variety, is not just a philosophical tendency; it is, in fact, a case of "ideophagy." What Unamuno means to do with ideas is to break them in, "like a pair of shoes, using them and making them mine." As a system of ideas, conventional pragmatism must (in its turn) be dealt with pragmatically; it must be dismantled, used, and, as Hegel would say, "absorbed." Unamuno is against any tyranny of ideas, even the tyranny of those ideas that pose as guides to action. The conventional pragmatist holds that knowledge is meaningless unless its goal is the fostering of life; however, in his preoccupation with life and its exigencies, he ends by bowing to a new idol. By so doing, he sacrifices what to Unamuno mattered most: our *own* life, pulsating beneath the jungle of ideas about it —that life made up of flesh and blood, but also of anguish, suffering, and hope.

The elimination of all idols is thus Unamuno's first step in the tireless search for himself and, through himself, for all human beings who like him enjoy or, in some instances, suffer an authentic life. Here we have the main motive for Unamuno's implacable blows against philosophies and "mere philosophers." Now, contrary to most of the "vitalist" and some of the "existentialist" philosophers, Unamuno did not think that the ideological idols were altogether useless. In his fight against "abstraction," Kiergegaard contended that anyone who thought as Hegel did, and identified being with thought, was less than human. Even more "existentialist" than Kierkegaard himself, Unamuno disagreed with this censure. For Unamuno, even the most abstract systems of thought were permeated with life. They were, in fact, one of man's ways of clinging to existence. Thus to Unamuno, Hegel seemed as human and as much concerned with his own concrete existence as those who expressed their concern more openly. Perhaps for Kierkegaard, living in solitude and anguish, only those who faced the fact of their own imminent annihilation could be saved, whereas for Unamuno, living in tragedy, fellowship, and hope, all could be saved, even those who insisted on substituting life and hope for thought.

Unamuno thoroughly criticized the philosophers' way of thinking, but only because this thinking frequently prevented the philosophers' recognizing what, irrevocably, they were, no matter how earnestly they might struggle to forget it: concrete, unique men of flesh and blood. Philosophers who attempt to reduce all realities to a single principle may try to account for the existence of human beings in purely rational terms, and in so doing they inevitably finish by turning concrete human beings into sheer abstractions. Although they often emphasize *the* life and *the* existence of men, they never succeed in reaching "*my* life" and "*my* existence." Unamuno could not help using formulas that are definitively impersonal in tone; he used language, and language cannot dispense with abstract terms. Thus, he wrote that the individual concrete life is "a principle of unity and a principle of continuity." But such words as 'principle' should not mislead us. Unamuno used the term 'principle', but he never identified it with an abstract "postulate." A principle was for him a kind of "fountain" or "spring," apt enough to describe the "source" of a number of human attitudes that are invariably concrete: the instinct of self-preservation, that of self-perpetuation, the awareness of tragedy, the experience of ambiguity, the inextricable mixture of desperation and hope, and so on. He felt that the "classical" philosophies had paid little attention to these attitudes. At best they tried to explain their nature, without meeting them face to face. But explanation is of no avail here; when everything has been accounted for, men realize that the most important things still remain unexplained. Philosophers,

Unamuno held, should begin by acknowledging that they are men, and so before they attempt to know "Truth" they ought to inquire about their own "truth."

The laborious search for that supreme reality, the man of flesh and blood, places Unamuno at a vantage point from which all vitalism and all existentialism seem mere theories about a reality that is so "pure" as to be hardly reality at all. But we must not imagine that in Unamuno's philosophical "point of departure" a "preoccupation with man" is at all synonymous with a "preoccupation with all that is human." In absolute contradistinction to Terence's famous dictum—*Homo sum et nihil humanum a mihi alienum puto*—Unamuno declared that humanity—the concept of humanity, that is—was foreign to him. Such a concept is as suspect as the concept of human existence with which philosophers attempt to disguise their lofty abstractions. That is why Unamuno, that tireless sapper of philosophies, began by proclaiming his desire to be the exact opposite of a philosopher in the classical or traditional sense of this word. This attitude was adopted as a consequence of his rather vague definition of "a philosopher." Unamuno defined "a philosopher" as "a man who above all else seeks truth," even when this truth forces him to acknowledge the lack of substantial, intimate reality in his own being—or the possibility of its final and complete annihilation in death. Because Unamuno refuses to be annihilated, he rebels against all the forces that contribute to man's destruction. One of these forces is reason, or rather the overemphasis on reason, which he defined, I am sorry to say, with the same lack of precision as the concept of philosopher. Nevertheless, it should be taken into account that Unamuno's rebellion against this supposed annihilation is nothing like a show of stubborn egocentrism. The man Unamuno speaks for is, of course, himself. Yet he also speaks for all men who are not—or cannot be—content with the fictitious comforts of rational philosophy. This includes, paradoxically, the rationalists themselves, for they are, along with everyone else, men of flesh and blood whose "being" cannot be compressed into any abstract concept, not even the concepts of "existence" and "life."

9   Ideas and ideals

Unamuno's pragmatic point of departure is thus so radical that it has often been misunderstood, occasionally even by Unamuno himself. He has insisted so much upon the predominance of the "concrete" as against the "abstract" that he has led his readers to believe that the "abstract"—ideas and reason—must be destroyed once and for all. Yet we must embrace pure ideas *as well,* provided that we do it as concretely existing beings for whom ideas are as necessary to life as life itself. As we shall see later on, men cannot dispense with the "reprisals against life" launched by ideas. For the worst of ideas is not what they really are—the opposites life clings to in order to exist—but what they often pretend to be: comforting explanations that conceal the pangs that accompanied their birth. Therefore, the man of flesh and blood, who thinks in order to live even when thinking confronts him with the fact that he must one day cease to exist, must not simply dismiss ideas and reasons as irrelevant and powerless. He must face these ideas; he must crack them open and penetrate them; he must above all discover the ideals that lie beneath them. In tune with some of Nietzsche's aphorisms, and perhaps influenced by them, Unamuno proclaimed that the substance of any idea is the ideal (the Desire, the Wish, the Will) held by the man who formulated it. Ideas possess an "essential truth," whereas ideals possess an "existential" truth. Even the most absurd of all ideals have a truth of their own that absurd ideas can never have. The brittle truth of a hundred birds on the wing belies the poor truth of a single bird in the hand. An idea may be declared to be true or false; an ideal is beyond the realm of truth and falsehood.

A series of startling paradoxes is the result of these reflections. To begin with, if ideals are the substance of ideas, it must be concluded that ideas have also, at bottom, an "existential" truth; otherwise, ideas could not even be conceived by men. Furthermore, a man of flesh and blood can more willingly accept (or rather, use) ideas than can some philosophers. Unamuno could not sympathize with the philosophers who importunately denounce the limitations of reason and of the ideas that reason produces.

The ideas that philosophers—including antirationalist philosophers—have circulated about man have ever been means of avoiding confrontation with this "man of flesh and blood," despite the fact that this "man" has given such ideas the only life they can ever possess. In defining "man" as "a rational being," "a thinking subject," "a historical reality," and so forth, philosophers have imagined themselves in touch with man's reality; actually, they have never been close to anything but a mere formal principle. And even if we define "man" as "an irrational creature," we will only succeed in laying down another principle, an abstract, philosophical postulate. Now, we should not concern ourselves just with the business of living, and leave sterile definitions to the philosophers. Notwithstanding his claims to the contrary, Unamuno's approach to man is still of a philosophical nature. It enters philosophy by the back door, but enters it nevertheless. In this respect Unamuno is indebted to a well-known tradition (the tradition of Saint Paul, Saint Augustine, Pascal, and Kierkegaard) which he himself has often acknowledged. The kinship exists, not because his philosophy is literally based on the works of these authors, but because it was in them that he discovered—most often, as with Kierkegaard, after his own position had been formulated—his true "spiritual brothers." But unlike most of them, Unamuno

did not want to enslave philosophy. Quite the contrary: he wanted
to free it from all idols, those of "irrationality" and "life" no less
than those of "reason" and "ideas." The motives for this double
objective are at the very heart of his thought, and cast a vivid
light on his conception of tragedy. For Unamuno it would be incorrect to speak of a man who existed authentically—in flesh and
blood—if he did not also exist tragically, and it would be inadequate to say that he lived tragically if his life were not continually
torn by the enmity—which acts through the coexistence—of two
series of warring provocations: the will to be, and the suspicion
that one can cease to be; feeling and thought; faith and doubt;
certainty and uncertainty; hope and desperation; heart and head;
or—in terms dear to some philosophers—life and logic.

10   Reason and faith

This enmity is the single but powerful source of man's fundamental tragic feeling: the feeling that his hope and faith are
incompatible with his reason, and yet cannot exist without it.
For reason subsists only by virtue of its constant war—and therefore its continual embrace—with hope and faith. We must avoid
the common error of supposing that Unamuno's thinking was
entirely slanted in favor of a complete victory of irrationality over
reason. Were this true neither could exist. Their warring coexistence is the substance of "tragedy," and the prime mover of
the "tragic sense of life." If men could entirely escape the so-
called "dictates of reason" to such an extent that they might
then be defined as "irrational beings" hungering for eternal life,
or blindly hopeful of it, there would be no tragedy in their existence. But Unamuno would then wonder whether they deserved to

be called "human" at all. For Unamuno, to live as a human being and to live tragically were one and the same thing.

It may be argued here that the question before us is a purely semantic one; that the identification of "human life" with "tragic life" is a linguistic convention that we may take or leave. But Unamuno does not ask anyone to assent to a proposition; he wants everyone to yield to a fact: the fact that the permanent tension between opposites, and especially between reason and the irrational, is the very core of existence.

There is little doubt, at any rate, that Unamuno would not agree with Leo Chestov's passionate descriptions of man as an essentially irrational creature. According to the Russian philosopher, every authentic human being must renounce all ties with the objective world in favor of his own world of dreams. As a consequence, man's private universe is not disturbed by reason or by the universal and necessary truths—the so-called "eternal truths"—that reason uncovers and formulates. On the other hand, the human universe that Unamuno describes is one in which the victory of dreams over reason is no less precarious than the victory of reason over dreams. It is a universe that offers no final respite, no quietude, no peace. Even when man is most entirely and happily immersed in the irrationality of his dreams, reason comes forward to trouble his life. And thus man comes to realize that the world of reason—of ideas and abstractions—must be cultivated for the sake of life no less than the world of dreams. The man of flesh and blood is not a person who turns from unreason and the dream world to embrace the implacable yet comforting light of reason, nor the person who escapes the rational universe to hide in the warm, trembling cosmos of faith, but one who vacillates incessantly between one and the other; a person who is, in fact, *composed of these two elements.*

Instead of being principles from which to deduce and define a concrete existence, these two worlds are perfectly alive, active almost pulsating realities. Unamuno has at times called them metaphorically, "whirlpools." And the man of flesh and blood, who lives at war with himself and never relinquishes his desire for peace, appears astride them both, sinking out of sight between them only to rise uncertainly again.

To claim that man must philosophize in order to live is not, therefore, just another formula; it is the faithful description of an experience. Unamuno's pragmatism, his invocation of utility, his insistence that truth tends to become veracity and the idea, an ideal, are thus entirely compatible with his waging war against all things merely pragmatic. Though Unamuno wrote that "the so-called innate desire to know only awakens and becomes active after the desire to know-in-order-to-live is satisfied," he did so only to emphasize, against the rationalists, the importance of irrationality. He also wrote, and here against irrationalists, that "the demands of reason are fully as imperious as those of life."

11   A world of tensions

Because he manifests a revolt of naturalism against the idealism of reason, and of the idealism of reason against pragmatical materialism, all attempts to pigeonhole Unamuno in one definite philosophical system are bound to fail. Unamuno does not advocate the union—which would entail a reconciliation, and eventually, a truce—of life and reason within the framework of a system where the idea of harmony would forever preclude any discord. There can be no harmony in that war which each human being wages against himself and his antagonists, but only perpetual strife, interminable contradiction, and continual—and fruitful— incivility. This is the only "formal principle," if that is the proper name for it, which permeates Unamuno's thinking. It may be stated as follows: To be, is to be against one's self.

Unamuno's emphasis on opposition, tension, and contradiction is obviously related to that type of thinking which since Hegel has been customarily called "dialectical." Nevertheless, there are two important differences between the conventional dialectical systems and Unamuno's.

On the one hand, dialectical systems attempt to describe and explain the attributes of the Cosmos as an impersonal being. In such systems, human reality follows the pattern of the cosmic reality. Sometimes "the Reality" is identified with "God," but even then the impersonal traits prevail over the personal ones. Unamuno's dialectic, however, is of an entirely personal nature. Unamuno refers mainly, if not exclusively, to human existence. And when the ideas of God and world are introduced, they are endowed with human characteristics. Even when he uses such abstract terms as 'reason' and 'the irrational', they are to be understood as embodied in unique, concrete human beings.

On the other hand, all the philosophers who have tried to describe reality as a dialectical process of some sort—Nicholas of Cusa and Giordano Bruno no less than Hegel—have built conceptual systems in which the opposites end in a reunification in the bosom of some ultimate and all-embracing principle. The war between particulars finds peace in the absolute generality of the essential One, so that the principle of identity overcomes, in the end, all contradictions. The dialectical method is one in which— as in Hegel—the total, "superior" truth (philosophical truth) reconciles the partial, "inferior" truths (mathematical and historical truth), one which purports to "save" all within the frame of the Absolute—the only realm in which peace is to be found. But in Unamuno's world, animated by the principle of perpetual civil war and unending strife, there is no place for any final harmony— and still less, any identity—which would be, in his opinion, the

equivalent of death. Among those thinkers who defended the dialectical approach, there was something akin to a headlong rush
toward the very identity they denounced, their attempts to dissem-
ble their own longing for an ultimate unity by calling it an "identity of opposites" notwithstanding. In Unamuno there is not the
slightest eagerness to be absorbed in this identity, nor the least
desire to pour the past into the future; there is just an everlasting
will to abide, "to prolong this sweet moment, to sleep in it, and
in it become eternal (*eternizarse*)." Unamuno wishes to prolong
his "eternal past" because only the moment most perfectly expresses what he seeks: a sense of being a man of flesh and blood
among other men of flesh and blood, yet still longing to be all
that one can long to be, to be "all in all and forever," a finite
individual and an infinite reality at the same time.

All identity or even harmony of opposites, all mere submersion of the moment in an intemporal eternity, is undone in
the perpetual battle between heart and head. So, for the authentic
man, the correct spiritual disposition is not belief in the impossible
simply because it is impossible (as some irrationalists would urge),
nor yet disbelief because of its impossibility (as most rationalists
would recommend), but its affirmation without believing it or, as
Unamuno said, by creating it. This is the only means of arriving at
that point where man is permitted to walk the floor of the abyss,
that "terrible substructure of tragedy and faith," which is the
common ground for both skeptics and believers, and where desperation ("the noblest, most profound, most human, and most fecund
state of mind") meets and fraternally embraces hope. The embrace
is a tragic one, and for Unamuno this means a vital one: a menace
of death and a fountain of life. Desperation and doubt can never
attain a complete victory over hope and belief, but the reverse is
also true. At a time when sentiment and belief ride roughshod
over reason and doubt, "there are reprisals," with "damned logic"
clinging, at the same time, to what we may well call "damned

feelings." And so the battle goes on forever: reason and faith, doubt and belief, thought and feeling, fact and desire, head and heart are united by an association in war, the only apposition in which they can survive since "each lives on the other," and feeds on the other, there being no third party to rejoice in or benefit from the struggle, no absolute unity or supreme harmony to lay peace between the antagonists. The only attainable peace lies in the eye of this powerful hurricane, but the eye subsists only because the hurricane moves on.

Thus the man of flesh and blood, who seemed to be so plain, simple, and straightforward, becomes a most complex reality seething with confusion and contradiction. No sooner had the philosopher asserted the concrete character of this creature then he injects it with what appears to be infinitely removed from any concrete reality: the pursuit of the impossible, the life of wish and dream. But even though the boundaries of personal unity seem thus to be broken, man never surrenders himself to any absolute being or to any transcendent realm of values. The man of flesh and blood strives to be all in all, while he fights to remain within the limits of his personal unity. He wishes to preserve his own nontransferable self, for being all in all means an infinite expansion of one's own personality rather than ceasing to be what one is.

At any rate, it would be a mistake to enlist Unamuno in the ranks of classical idealism, as it would be inadequate to consider him a naturalist or a realist. To be sure, Unamuno speaks often of "realism," but at such times it is to be understood as an injunction to create reality rather than as an invitation to describe it faithfully and accurately. Also he seems sometimes on the brink of naturalism and even materialsm, but it is only because he wishes to emphasize what is concrete in man's existence. Realism, naturalism, and materialism define man in terms of what he is, which nearly always means, in terms of what he has been. Idealism, on the other hand, defines man in terms of what he ought to be.

Unamuno prefers to "define" him in terms of what he will become, or more exactly, in terms of what he wants to become, since "we are lost or saved on the basis of what we wanted to be, and not for what we have been." If a name could be given to Unamuno's philosophical anthropology, "poetic realism" would perhaps be the least inadequate of all.

12   Man as a dreamer

In view of the above, it is only too natural that Unamuno's notion of man should be drawn more successfully in his novels than in his philosophical essays. In Unamuno's novels there is frequent use of such expressions as 'living, suffering flesh', 'the marrow of bone', and 'the panting of the soul'. There is frequent mention of dreams, since it is through dreams that the creatures we imagine, exist. We may say, then, that in the characters of these novels Unamuno's conception of man is truly given flesh. And this, as he writes, "without recourse to theatrical scenery, or other tidbits of realism which invariably lack the true, eternal reality, that of personality." All the "characters" thus described—or, more correctly speaking, created—struggle in order to exist. They fight against everybody, including their author, in order to be men of flesh and blood, for only in the course of such a struggle can they achieve their greatest reality.

Like their creator, all are "men of contradictions," and their goal in life is to "carve themselves a soul." *Mist*'s (*Niebla*) Augusto Pérez goes so far as to threaten his author. He cannot do it, as the latter can, "with a stroke of his pen"—after all, the character is not an author. But he can menace the author by reminding him that God—a sort of supreme author—may stop dreaming him. As we shall see later on, the so-called fictitious characters in the novels possess a reality of their own. To be sure, they are the consequence of their author's "dreams." But their creator depends on his characters as much as they depend on him. Thus, Unamuno wants to make clear that although each man— "real" or "fictitious"—is truly himself, he cannot live without the others. Unamuno's repeated insistence on the notions of the "dream" and "being dreamed" may be grounded, of course, in his undeniable fondness for paradox; it is indeed a paradox to say that real persons and fictitious characters in novels are equally "men of flesh and blood." But underlying Unamuno's witticisms and puns there is a serious attempt to show that personality is more basic to men—real or fictitious—than any of the other characteristics of human existence thus far devised by philosophers. There is, and most important, the wish to show that all men of flesh and blood are closely interrelated. The so-called "independence" of the solitary man—again, "real" or "fictitious"—is deceptive. "A solitary dream," Unamuno writes, "is illusion, appearance; a dream shared is truth and reality." As Augusto Pérez says to his dog, Orfeo, "The world is the dream we all have in common, the 'communal dream'."

If we say that the fictitious characters in novels are, in a sense, real, we can also say that real men are fictitious creatures —characters in a kind of cosmic novel. They too are the products of a dream: God's dream. This is the origin of the anguish felt by man as he becomes aware of the vast dream in which he is immersed, and of the possibility that some day he will awaken; that is, become convinced of the ephemeral nature of his dream, thereby sinking into the "twilight of logic and ratiocination," which can offer no consolation to "the hearts of those condemned to the dream of life." Because the awakening from this dream means that we cease to exist, we implore our Author not to stop dreaming us with a strange prayer: "Dream us, Our Lord!"

Now, just as faith lacks vigor without doubt, and hope becomes sterile without desperation, so we are here confronted with the breathtaking paradox that dream lacks substance without the possibility of awakening from it and rebelling against it. When we rebel against the fact that God is constantly dreaming us, we assist God in His everlastingly creative task—dreaming.

The assistance we render God, analogous to that rendered us by our fictional heroes, makes it possible that just as we are God's children, He is, as Unamuno proclaimed, our child, the child "of poor anguished humanity, since in us the eternal, infinite, Universal Consciousness manifests itself, exists incarnate." As a consequence, the relationship between God and His creations is not one of cause and effect and even less one of action and consequence, but a peculiar relationship best described as "that of dreamer and dreamed." Perhaps this explains why Unamuno surmised that far from being products of a necessary emanation or an arbitrary creation, we are products of a dream. We are not, however, entirely at the mercy of the Dreamer, for we have the power of changing His dreams. We thus dream while awake, being both the object of those dreams in which we are the "creatures" and the subject of those dreams in which the world of what we call "fiction" comes alive.

13   God and the world

Should we say, then, that we have in the notion—or rather, the metaphor—of the dream the unifying principle of the man of flesh and blood, the meeting point of all tensions and all oppositions, the "absolute essence" of human reality and, for that matter, of all reality? If we are God's dreams, and God himself is our dream, can we not conclude that dream is the universal stuff of which all things are made?

It goes without saying that Unamuno does not answer these questions as a philosopher would. He does not use argument, let alone any sort of rigorous proof. He uses a confusing but stimulating method in which bold assertions are blended with series of interrogations. As an example of bold assertion, let me quote the following: "It is not my fragile and transitory self, which feeds upon the earth and upon which the earth will one day feed that must be victorious, but my true eternal self, my archetype and form since before and until after time, the idea that God, the Universal Consciousness, has of me"—a rather surprising statement, excessively Platonic for one who has so often argued against "ideas," "forms," and "archetypes." The examples of interrogations are so numerous that I need cite no example. But it is illuminating to see that many of them refer to the question of dreams—in the aforementioned sense—and the relationship between "a dreamer" and "that which he dreams." This shows that Unamuno was certain about the real nature of this universal tissue of dreams, and in particular about the role that the Great Dreamer plays in the economy of the universe. If, on the one hand, everything seems to move, in his opinion, toward the Dreamer, on the other hand he maintains that even in His bosom there is conflict, tension, and contradiction—or, to use Unamuno's own terms, strife, struggle, and war.

Since God is the perpetrator of all fecund war, He could be truly called "The Eternalizer," rather than "The Eternal." The war in which all things live has also its roots in the divine reality. Unamuno opposes, then, both rationalists who worship the principle of identity and irrationalists who rejoice in contradiction, so far as all of them agree that God is the Reality in which all opposition is reconciled and all diversity unified. He also opposes those Platonic—and Neoplatonic—philosophies that reduce the sensible world to the status of a copy and reflection of the intelligible world. According to these philosophies, the authentic life consists in a contemplation of the divine world of the Idea. But since such a life would of necessity be a disembodied existence—or, more exactly, would mean living *as though* one led a disembodied existence—the Platonic emphasis on intelligibility and unity always ends by sacrificing the concrete man who formulated—and longed for—it. An analogous situation occurs, by the way, in those philosophies that, while apparently hostile to the idea of a static intelligible world, are no less eager to set the torch to the particular and the concrete, even though they concoct theories about a supposedly dynamic unity of opposites. Unamuno called these philosophies "monistic catchpennies," because although their main premise is the existence of diversity, in the end (as with Nicholas of Cusa, Giordano Bruno, and Hegel), this same diversity is seen to be the stuff of which unity is made. The proponents of these pseudomonistic systems hailed the idea of contradiction, but soon allowed their thoughts to be permeated by a principle of identity. All that is not identity, claimed Giordano Bruno, is vanity, nothingness, illusion, and void. All oppositions, proclaimed Hegel, must be reconciled. The absolute One, the absolute Idea, the pure Identity, thus emerge victorious over all opposition, so much so that in the end all struggles to win an eternal peace are resolved. Peace is at last attained, but with it, Unamuno argued, life itself comes to an end.

There is no reconciliation and no peace in Unamuno's truly dynamic universe, whether it includes only the minds of men or also that of God. Here war plays the part of the Heraclitean "father of all things." But although Heraclitus admitted the existence of a certain cosmic rhythm—the rhythmic alternation according to which the universe travels an Upward and Downward Way—Unamuno dissociates existence from anything that might for so much as an instant diminish its unbending "fury." What we term "peace" is found only in war. Thus unity and identity are both present in Unamuno's universe. But they exist, as much as anything does, within the framework of an unending battle. They struggle to hold their ground, and they push forward—though unsuccessfully—toward ultimate domination. If God can be called the "Universal Consciousness," as Unamuno has sometimes named Him, it is not because He is the World's Reason, but only because He wages an unending struggle to merge with the world—and at the same time to free Himself from it.

It would of course be impertinent to ask Unamuno for any rational elucidation of a theme that, more than any other, he has always left adrift in a sea of indefiniteness and paradox. If, on the one hand, Unamuno surmised that this Universal Consciousness is trapped in matter, thus seeming to adhere to a pantheistic and even materialistic monism, on the other hand he declared that God—the eternal and infinite consciousness of the world—is something transcendent. In either event it can be said that He is *in* the battle. Could we not even say that He *is* the battle—or the very symbol of it? At any rate, as soon as we try to divorce Him from any struggle we are in danger of depriving Him of His existence. Then too, this battle presupposes a constant suffering after the manner of Schopenhauer—who probably influenced Unamuno more than the latter would have been willing to admit. It presupposes that anguish that is the "only truly mysterious mystery" and seems to rise as if it were a cosmic sap from inorganic matter through man to that Person submerged in matter who is its eternal and infinite consciousness. We might almost conclude that each man, each thing, each activity, and even each concept is a member of a sort of "body mystic" tormented by that anguish that is an essential part of the "God who suffers" and is as much a consolation to His creatures as it is to Himself. We are here confronted with a symbiosis of a very particular type—a cosmic symbiosis that concepts such as "interaction," "reciprocal action," and "mutual dependence" can never adequately describe. And yet we are in touch with something quite like an "organic symbiosis" when we read that "in God's bosom consciousnesses are born and die—die?—their births and deaths constituting His life," and especially when we read that "when we say God eternally produces things, and things eternally produce God, we are repeating ourselves."

Are we justified in saying that after all Unamuno returns to those very same definitions and formulae which the panentheists of all periods circulated so monotonously? Only if we fail to notice that he at once weakens his definitions and formulae by voicing them in a series of unanswered questions. The method of interrogation of which I spoke before now gains an upper hand. Might not matter itself, Unamuno asks, be the beginning of the unconscious God? Is not God the end rather than the beginning of the universe? Is there a difference in terms of eternity between beginning and end? Are things ideas of the Master Consciousness? Does God the Eternalizer ever forget what He has once thought? Questions of this kind result from a natural dissatisfaction with any definite solution, and show again how pointless is any attempt to contain Unamuno in a single intellectual pigeonhole. Monism, pantheism, materialism, spiritualism, and personalism are some of the best-known responses to the above questions. Not one of them is, however, entirely acceptable to Unamuno. God is "the ideal of humanity," "man projected to the infinite power and eternalized in it," but He is also that Highest Person who transcends this human projection, who affirms Himself over and against it. He is the reason of the world and its unreason, its consciousness and unconsciousness, its anguish and pleasure, its spirit and matter. Thus the only really apt name for God is what Unamuno was finally to give Him: "my heretic God." So much a heretic that He looks upon Himself with an heretical eye. God, like man, doubts Himself and in the process of doubting creates both Himself and man. This seems to be the meaning implied in "Atheism" and "The

Atheist's Prayer," two of Unamuno's sonnets which best reveal his sense of the Divine. If in the first he says that:

> God is the unattainable
> desire we have to be Him; Who
> knows? Perhaps God Himself
> is an atheist;

in the second the atheist prays to a God in whom he cannot rationally believe, but whose existence he must affirm unless he wishes to deny his own. That is why this strange atheist exclaims:

> Because of You I suffer,
> Inexistent God, since if You existed
> I too would really exist.

This is the God who denies and affirms Himself, who desires and fears, who pulsates in the heart of mankind and hovers above it. A God who defies rational proof but welcomes those who approach Him armed with the tools of belief and love. This last point is all-important, since a "belief in God begins with the desire that there be a God, with the inability to live without Him." Such a longing for God is no mere desire—at least, not one that thought can assuage; it is more in the nature of an anguish, a yearning for Him. He who dreams the world is in turn its dream; the Eternalizer is Himself eternalized. Without man and the world, God would not exist. But without God, man and the world would founder in the nightmare of the void from which the only salvation is an unending dream, the perennial memory of the "Master Dreamer." Nietzsche had proclaimed that "God is dead." Unamuno maintains that even the death of God is the life of man.

THREE

Immortality – The Tragedy of Christianity –
The Idea of History

14 The hunger for immortality

BY ANY STANDARDS of religious or philosophical orthodoxy Unamuno's idea of God was a "heretical" one. He refused to apply any of the conventional philosophical categories—"actuality" and "potentiality," "being" and "nonbeing," or "essence" and "existence"—to God. The reasons for this theological and philosophical "heresy" are deeply embedded in his view that all beings tend to sink into the vortex of an unending polemic, a permanent struggle. Since tragedy stirs in the depths of everything, it is also active in the depths of God, whose life is as full of tension and conflict as the life of man and that of the universe.

On this grandiose and turbulent stage, and subject to the same dynamic impulse, Unamuno's other major themes unfold— his other major obsessions; and the most insistent of them all is that of immortality. Its role is such a central one that at times it threatens to obscure all the rest. Faced with the question, "What

is the most important problem for man?" Unamuno would have
declared, in all likelihood, that it was the question of the soul's
ultimate destiny, that is, whether or not the soul is immortal. Although, in phrasing the question, he often used the vocabulary
of the Platonic-Christian tradition, his purpose was not the same.
In fact, it is misleading to speak of Unamuno's idea of the soul
in any terms that suggest an entity separate, or separable, from
the body. Even though we shall be obliged to use this same
terminology, as Unamuno was—the "Soul," "immortality," and
"immortality of the soul"—it must be remembered that the real
problem that concerned Unamuno was that of the individual human
death. Was each man doomed to an eternal death, or could one
hope to survive it? This was the obsessive question in Unamuno's
concern with the problem of the immortality of the soul.

Unamuno could not avoid thinking of death as both inevitable
and frightening. His struggle against the fear of death was so
impassioned that in dealing with the problem of immortality he
seems to have halted the incessant pendulum movement of his
thought at one of its extremes. If in speaking of God and man,
negation unfailingly accompanied affirmation, doubt, faith, and
despair, hope, in Unamuno's talk of immortality, assent often
triumphed over denial. We are tempted to conclude that his
desire for immortality blinded him to the misery of death, and
that in this instance his heart won its only victory over the mind.

But such a conclusion would be premature, for to the degree
that it was authentic—and it most probably was—Unamuno's
belief in immortality was also beset by doubt. There can be no
other explanation for his frequent use of the expression 'hunger
for immortality' instead of 'belief in immortality'—'hunger' being
an obviously much less intellectual term than 'belief'. We believe
in immortality, Unamuno surmised, primarily because we desire
it. Our desire to be immortal, to survive, is even stronger than
our desire that there be a God. The hunger for immortality is an

almost physiological impulse. Reason teaches us that immortality is highly problematical, if not absurd. Or, to be more exact, reason teaches us nothing in this connection, and thus leaves us in a state of perplexity. That is more disturbing than the certainty of our death. We can accept the Platonic proofs of the immortality of the soul only when we blindly accept their premises—if all that is "simple" does not perish, and if the soul is simple, then the soul does not perish. The premises themselves cannot be proved, either rationally or empirically. Therefore, although reason is in this instance "neutral," it often leads us into skepticism. It is a very peculiar kind of skepticism, one that acts as a stimulant rather than as a palliative. The stronger the conviction that immortality cannot be proved, the more deeply belief in immortality penetrates our minds. But the hunger for survival is tied to the anxiety caused by the imaginative anticipation of death as a complete extinction of our being.

Although Unamuno's thought on the problem of immortality was largely dependent upon Christian theological notions, it was not subservient to them. He struggled against these notions as much as, if not more than, he accepted them. Therefore, let us analyze the meaning of 'immortality' in Unamuno's thought and compare and contrast it with the "immortalities" of the theological and philosophical systems.

To begin with, Unamuno's "definition" of immortality is extremely vague: a thing is immortal when it is limitless in both time and being. 'To be immortal' means to be—or perhaps rather to wish to be—all in all *per omnia saecula saeculorum*. Unamuno's conception of immortality is related to the notion of impetus, or *conatus*, which, according to Spinoza (frequently cited by Unamuno in this respect), "impels" all things to the conservation of their own being. The essence of immortality seems to be, therefore, the struggle to perpetuate one's self. But although Unamuno was extremely sympathetic to the Spinozian notion of *conatus*, he disagreed with Spinoza in one important respect. Spinoza maintained that *nos experimur aeternos esse,* that "we feel that we are eternal." As François Meyer has pointed out, however, Unamuno adopts only Spinoza's verbal expression, and makes it serve his own end, quite unlike Spinoza's. As Meyer says, this end is a kind of "ontological greediness." Immortality is not only a *conatus* directed toward one's own being; it is an impetus to participate in all the other beings while remaining one and the same. Furthermore, immortality must be understood in its widest connotation and not limited to the desire felt by one human individual to survive. All things, and not only human beings, "long" to endure by absorbing the entire universe into themselves. And when this proves impossible, they "prefer" to be absorbed by the whole rather than remain confined within their own being.

Immortality is, then, a universal "desire" and one that never limits itself in any way. Being immortal means being both one's self and all that is not the self at the same time and forever. It can easily be seen that this "definition" of immortality is based upon the refusal to sacrifice anything. Properly speaking, for Unamuno, to be immortal is to be God. But the impossibility of any finite being's attaining this end leads Unamuno to place the following implicit "restrictions" upon the idea of immortality: (1) immortality is considered to be predominantly "human immortality"; (2) emphasis is placed more and more upon the survival of the human individual as individual, even if this means a diminishing, rather than an expansion of his being; (3) all possible forms of survival are explored, even the most "unsatisfactory" ones if these are found to be more "verifiable" than others. Thus, the "ontological greediness" originally ascribed to every being is so severely curtailed that we may wonder why Unamuno considered this "greediness" the basic metaphysical drive of all realities. It is still possible, however, to see in this "greediness" at least a general tendency—perhaps a "limiting concept." The innermost core of Unamuno's longing for immortality is still the impetus toward an ontological amplification of individuality and particularity, with each thing in the universe "longing" to become "all in all" and forever. But if a thing cannot be all things for all time, let it be at least itself most of the time. And if man cannot be God, let him at least share in imagination the eternality and omnipresence of God.

The longing for immortality itself oscillates perpetually between a maximum and a minimum. The maximum is "to be all in all while being one's self." The minimum is to subsist and survive, no matter how. This minimum plays an important role in Unamuno's thinking on immortality. Very often he seems to conceive of immortality as man's longing to endure and nothing more; it need only help him to overcome the fear of death. Thus, when no other alternative seems available, Unamuno is willing to accept an idea of immortality which presupposes a sacrifice of individuality and a submersion in a single (ubiquitous) existence. Faced with a choice between a simple annihilation and absorption by a universal reality (God, Nature, Mankind), Unamuno would certainly favor the latter. He would resign himself to a "survival" in the undifferentiated reservoir of an Absolute, even if this Absolute were, like the Buddhist Nirvana, the nearest thing to "Nothingness." For the Buddhistic idea of "Nothingness"—similar to the ideas of absolute Will and pure Unconsciousness proposed by Schopenhauer or Eduard von Hartmann—implies some kind of existence; in fact, for those who believe in it, or dream of it, it is true existence as opposed to the falsehood of the individual self, which always dissolves into transitory elements. We may, for the sake of universal Life, sacrifice our private life; we may, for the sake of the Absolute, abandon the relative. To be sure, Nirvana is a lesser evil with which Unamuno could only begrudgingly content himself. But it would still be something. "Something is better than nothing" is Unamuno's commonsensical recommendation when the question of the survival of human beings is at stake.

15   The forms of immortality

Unamuno agrees, then, with all those who long for, or preach, immortality, but he disagrees with the specific content of any of the innumerable doctrines of survival outlined by religious thinkers and philosophers. The doctrines of Buddha, of Schopenhauer, and of Eduard von Hartmann are, in a way, soothing. They are not, however, sufficient, and least of all, convincing. A detailed analysis of Unamuno's feelings about the various Greek doctrines of "immortality" (Orphic, Platonic, Aristotelian, etc.) would result in similar instances of agreement followed immediately by confessions of dissatisfaction. As an illustration, let us select one such doctrine, and imagine Unamuno's reaction to it.

This is the doctrine—or rather, eclectic combination of doctrines—according to which 'to be immortal' means both "to be actual" and "to be eternal." To be actual is, properly speaking, to be what one essentially is, to fulfill all of one's own potentialities. To be eternal is to transcend time, or rather, to contain in one's bosom all possible time. Not all beings are immortal to the same degree. Some come into existence and then pass away, in accordance with the "law" of generation and corruption; others come close to immortality in that their movements approach the perfect circular movement; other beings—some would say only the Prime Mover—are truly immortal, because they are purely actual. From potentiality to actuality, from temporality to eternity, from imperfection to perfection, there is a hierarchy of being that is also a hierarchy of value. In one sense it can be said that each being in such a universe "desires" to be itself, to occupy its place in the ontological and axiological hierarchy, each partaking of immortality according to its degree of actuality and perfection. It is a beautiful and well-ordered cosmos, and one that is likely to assuage some philosophers' fears of annihilation. So far as this doctrine promotes the idea of immortality, and is even based upon it, it would be acceptable to Unamuno. But as soon as he had found a modicum of consolation in it, he would rebel against the many limitations it implied. For the immortality hinted at in this seemingly perfect universe lacks anguish, anxiety, and drama. Furthermore, this immortality is given, not won. If no other immortality were available, Unamuno would say, we may accept this one. But not without protest, for if it sometimes appeals to our minds, it can never seduce our hearts.

There is, then, no concept of immortality which completely satisfies Unamuno. But there is at least one concept of immortality near which he seems to linger: the Christian one. As a matter of fact, he often tackled the problem of immortality and the problem of Christianity simultaneously, as if they were interchangeable. "The hunger for immortality" and "the agony of Christianity" are two dimensions of the same *magna quaestio.*

True enough, Christian thinkers—if I may be permitted a few quick passes at such a complex subject—have often treated the question of immortality in a way that elicited particular reservations from Unamuno. So far as they followed certain intellectual patterns outlined by some Greek philosophers—above all, the Platonists—Christian thinkers have always severely limited the idea of immortality. These limitations concern not only time, but also being; instead of claiming that "the man of flesh and blood" is immortal, these thinkers claimed that the soul is immortal. This viewpoint is already apparent in some of the "eleventh-hour" Greek philosophies, particularly those which, like Neoplatonism, can be shown to have emphasized the central role of the soul in the economy of the universe. The philosophers of these schools provided so many arguments for it that many of the conceptual instruments later employed by Christian authors in dealing with immortality were drawn from these late Greek sources. Consequently, one may wonder why Unamuno was more satisfied with the Christian concept of immortality than with the Hellenic one. Yet, there is one point in the Christian concept—and even when most influenced by Greek philosophy—which probably attracted Unamuno's interest, and that was the fact that this concept is not at all a Christian elaboration of a series of Greek arguments, but rather a dynamic symbiosis of the two. The relation between Greek philosophy and Christianity was, Unamuno declared again and again, one of struggle: "Christianity, that irrational faith in which Christ came to life in order to give us new life, was saved by the rationalistic culture of Greece, which was in turn saved by Christianity." This is, in Unamuno's vocabulary, an "agonizing relationship," and one that cannot be avoided, for "a purely rationalistic tradition is as impossible as a purely religious tradition." Because of this struggle, the Christian concept of the immortality of the soul must have appeared to Unamuno, on closer consideration, considerably less "limited" than the Hellenic concept. It is still concerned, to a large degree, with the immortality of the "soul," but this soul is no longer comparable to an idea; it is the soul of a person—of a "man of flesh and blood," who wants to perpetuate himself not only with his mind, but with all his being.

To be sure, a few Greek thinkers—in particular, those influenced by Neoplatonism—had some inkling of a more "dynamic" immortality than the pure actuality and eternality of ideas would allow. They defined the soul as the only outstanding dynamic reality in motion upon the basically motionless stage of the universe, the only substance able to ascend—and descend—the ladder that leads through the various elements of the great cosmic hierarchy known as the "Great Chain of Being." For the soul to be immortal, these thinkers argued, it had only to strive to be so. This soul finds rest only in the world of ideas. But it is not itself an idea, an impassive entity; it moves ceaselessly upward or down-ward, always anxious to live a God-like life, but never attaining it. Therefore, in this idea of the soul, Unamuno found a mode of being which greatly attracted him: a state of tension, a permanent undercurrent of anxiety. Unfortunately, as soon as the soul had been "defined" in this way, the everpresent intellectualism of the Greek philosophical tradition gained the upper hand. The life of the soul was considered basically "theoretical," and "contemplative," even though the soul's continual state of contemplation —or its aspiration toward it—was disguised with the misleading name of "activity." Therefore, the Hellenic idea of immortality (and the Christian idea so far as it was influenced by the former) was, in Unamuno's word, a "caricature" of the "true immortality." If the man of flesh and blood is identified with the soul, and if the soul is defined in terms of such predicates as "rational" and "contemplative," then the immortality of the soul will be little more than an immortality of reason. This was, incidentally, what some Greek thinkers came to believe when they declared that only the so-called "Active Intellect"—or "Universal Reason"— was truly immortal. We are immortal not as individuals, but only as participants in the one and only Active Intelligence whose infinite rays of light permeate everything that is rational in this world.

Christian thinkers have never subscribed to an idea of immortality that goes so far as to deny personal immortality; the Alexandrian and Averroistic doctrines of the "Active Intellect" as the only immortal "soul" have always encountered the bitterest opposition among Christian philosophers. Yet, the concept of a suprapersonal immortality is one of the two extremes toward which Christian thought was forced by the Hellenic intellectual tradition. Unamuno emphasized this point again and again. Since Christian thinkers cannot dispense with reason, they must acknowledge some of the consequences that a rational approach to the problem would produce. One such consequence is that whenever a thing is im-

mortal it must at the same time be universal and rational. On the
other hand, Christian thinkers are committed to the doctrine of
personal immortality, whether rational or not. They have to affirm
what their reason may deny; they must struggle against reason
while they are obliged to embrace it. They cannot use reason to
prove immortality, but they can use it to strengthen hope and
faith through doubt.

   This is why Unamuno sharply opposed both the rational
"proofs" of immortality and the idea that immortality is restricted
to the "immaterial soul." He found support for his views in a
very influential "tradition" of Christian thinkers; the theologians
and philosophers he preferred in this connection were not Saint
Thomas Aquinas or Cardinal Cajetan, but Saint Paul and Saint
Augustine (and those laymen, Pascal and Kierkegaard, and perhaps Kant). The soul they spoke of was not an impassive entity,
but just the contrary: a purely personal, radically intimate being,
capable of possessing—of enjoying or suffering—experiences, an
entity that stumbled and regained its feet, sinned and repented,
and, above all, hated and loved. Instead of simply detaching itself
from the body, freeing itself, in a Platonic manner, as if from a
prison, or living in the body as if it were outside of it, this soul
dragged the body after it toward eternal life, making the body a
"spiritual" and not exclusively a rational one. These theologians
and philosophers believed in something that Greek thinkers would
have refused to admit for fear of betraying the rational spirit—
namely, the resurrection of the dead, what Saint Paul called divine
madness before the curious, but skeptical, Athenians in the
Areopage. These were the things Unamuno delighted in underlin-
ing and tossed, like bones of contention, in the teeth of all manner
of Pharisees. As a consequence, Unamuno completely rejected the
"scholastic tradition"—which, incidentally, he misinterpreted and
misjudged, for he identified it with Thomism, and Thomism with
the doctrine of the modern Scholastics who had diluted the theology

of Thomas Aquinas with large doses of Wolffianism. Unamuno's vehement forays against what he called "the theology of jurisprudence" (Thomism) were based upon this misinterpretation and oversimplification. Instead of denouncing Unamuno's historical errors, however, it would be better to understand what truths they were meant to reveal. One of these is quite obvious. Unamuno claimed that conceptualization and reason were necessary if the hunger for immortality was to perpetuate itself. The right type of reason could serve as both curb and goad. But this sort of reason was not to be found in Thomistic philosophy, not evident in Thomistic "proofs." Although Thomistic reason promoted a kind of fictitious security, it was only "an impotent Christianity," a "cathedral of adobe." That is why Unamuno was so vehement in his rejection of Thomistic conceptualization in favor of belief *and* reason, *and* the permanent war between them.

16   Immortality as a struggle

What, then, was the variety of immortality which Unamuno espoused? Nothing less than an "absolute immortality" firmly anchored in the depths of all things and unbounded by any qualifications. But the immortality that concerned him most was that of the human beings who longed for it. Thus the hunger for immortality becomes a "private hunger for survival" that causes each human to cry out in anguish: "I will not die!"—or at least to live as if he cried out so. Into this framework, reacting against the naïve believers and the mere reasoners, Unamuno reintroduced the tragic sense that he had discovered in connection with man and God. There is in the concept of immortality too a perpetual contradiction. For example, deep within the concept of immortality there is the "sense of mortality." It may be argued that this is a derivative sensation, since it is the result of reflection rather than instinct. But once the "sense of mortality" attaches itself to our life, there is no escaping it. The sense of our own mortality becomes then a common-sense truth. It shows us, as Vladimir Nabokov has pointedly written, that "our existence is but a brief crack of light between two eternities of existence"—a "personal glitter in the impersonal darkness" on both sides of one's life. The "sense of mortality" is, furthermore, strengthened by our reason, which can never definitively prove mortality or immortality, but which usually finds the former more probable and "reasonable" than the latter. When experience and common sense join forces with reason, the conclusion is inescapable: human death is a certainty, and immortality at best an illusion. The denial of immortality, or the impossibility of proving it, is, therefore, the virtual equivalent of the affirmation of death. But, as Unamuno says, the "yes" lives on the "no." Or, more accurately, man's life swings between the "yes" and the "no." This oscillation of judgment does not, however, lead us to a skeptical "suspension of all judgment"; but rather leads us to a permanent restlessness. It is another manifestation of the perpetual struggle of opposites which touches off the cosmic "civil war" in the midst of which all things live.

If he realizes the deep meaning of this "ontological oscillation," man can neither completely despair when faced with the certainty of his death, nor have absolute confidence in the security of his survival. "The immortal origin of the longing for immortality," Unamuno has written, "is a despairing resignation and a resigned despair." Therefore, to live is "to agonize"—in the etymological sense of 'to agonize' so insistently emphasized by Unamuno: "to fight against death." Although we are "in agony," we are never completely overcome by death. To be sure, we are never completely victorious either. But that is precisely what we want, Unamuno surmises, and what prevents us from dying once and for all. Even if there actually were a survival after death, it would be a continuation of the struggle against the threat of death. Without this "agony," the idea of immortality would be unbearable —if at all conceivable. The very idea of survival in Hell is less distressing to Unamuno than the idea of an eternal death disguised as an eternal and soporific bliss: "It is better to live in pain," he writes, "than to continue to live in peace." Unamuno's ideal of survival and immortality seems a kind of eternal purgatory where suffering and anxiety mingle with bliss and hope. Life on earth, incidentally, is just such a purgatory; it is the best possible exemplification of the aforementioned "agony." For, ultimately, the true life is *this* life; the rest is silence—or perhaps "mere literature." It is only too deplorable that this life is not eternal. Accordingly, "the immortality we crave is a phenomenal immortality"; we want the "bulk and not the shadow of immortality." We want, Unamuno concludes, to survive as we are, and as we wish to be, with our body, our home, our friends, our familiar landscapes, with all the things we love and hate, and to be sure, with our own past.

Unamuno never ceased to emphasize the "agonizing" nature of life and, therefore, the "agonizing" nature of any possible survival. "A life without any death in it, without incessant deterioration," he writes, "would be nothing but perpetual death, a stony rest. Those who do not die, do not live; those who do not die each instant, who are not resurrected in the same instant, do not live, and those who do not doubt do not live." The beatific vision we are promised as a reward would soon become a punishment if it did not entail "a labor, a continual and never-ending conquest of the Supreme and Infinite Truth, a hungry diving and delving ever more deeply into the bottomless depths of Eternal Life." Here Unamuno coincides with Lessing (and perhaps with most Romantics): the unceasing conquest of Truth is better than Truth

itself. The Kingdom of God "endures force"; we must abandon the
pseudotranquilizing certainty that it will simply be given us,
whether for merit or through grace. If such a Kingdom were not
always on the verge of being lost it would be a kingdom of the
dead and not of the living. "Not to die" means to struggle in order
to escape death, to live restlessly, fully aware of the danger that
God may stop thinking us—no longer dream us. Unamuno does
not ask for beatitude or for the complete fulfillment of hope; he
asks for a Kingdom of "hopeful dissatisfaction, or of dissatisfied
hope." "My soul, at least," he wrote, "yearns for something else,
not absorption, nor quiet, nor peace, nor extinction, but an eternal
drawing closer without ever arriving, an endless longing, an eternal
hope eternally renewed"—in short, "an eternal Purgatory rather
than a Celestial bliss; an eternal ascension." For "he who achieves
Supreme Truth will be absorbed by it and cease to exist." And
to avoid this cessation of existence—the worst of all evils, the
supreme evil—we must stand guard and work, instead of resting
in Paradise; we must "use eternity to conquer the bottomless abyss
of the bosom of God, hand over hand, eternally."

17   The eternal present

"Bosom of God," "Supreme Truth," "eternal ascension"—these
expressions recur often in Unamuno's writings. Nevertheless, it
would be a mistake to suppose that his longings for immortality
are always expressed in this lofty language. Immortality can have
many forms, and Unamuno is not willing to sacrifice any of them.
He has described two of these forms with particular care:
the survival of one's past, and the survival of one's self in the
memory of others.

Most doctrines of immortality are geared to the future; they assert that man will go on living for ever, but say little, or nothing, about how man should face his past. The reason for this silence about the past is the supposedly beatific character of human survival; a complete state of bliss seems to entail absolute forgetfulness. But Unamuno finds such doctrines not to his liking. To be sure, he insists on continuation, but cannot conceive it without "recuperation." A living immortality, he thinks, is one that allows us to relive the experiences of the past—if not all experiences, at least the ones that constitute the basic stratum of our personality. Since no rational account can be given of this recovery of the past, Unamuno expresses the wish for it mainly in poetic discourse. In one of his poems he cried out for "the days of yesterday," and asked the "Father of Life" that the past for which "he longs" be returned to him "all gathered up in the end," and as alive as when it first took place. He wants to relive what he once lived. The end of the sonnet "My Heaven" is quite explicit on this point; gentle melancholy and willful longing mingle together in these lines:

> Toward an eternal yesterday direct my flight
> But do not let it arrive for, Lord, you have
> No other heaven that would half so fill me with joy.

It may seem surprising that Unamuno should emphasize "the past" when we take into account his condemnation of the "dead crust" of the past, and his insistence on "intralife" and "intra-history" (see chapter four). There may be some inconsistency here, and I will not try to remove it merely to show that Unamuno was more logical than he seemed. Perhaps he thought there was an authentic and an unauthentic past, and that only the former was worth recovering and worth being relived. Perhaps he merely wanted to express the wish that all that is—and, therefore, has been—should become "eternized" (a wish also expressed in his longing to "perpetuate the moment"). I think Unamuno's insistence on "recovery" and "reliving" has its origin in his desire not to confuse immortality with purely atemporal bliss. If immortality means temporal survival, it must not destroy time, but continually relive and reshape it. It is also possible that since experience and reason alike show that survival as indefinite continuation of one's self is highly improbable, Unamuno wanted to make certain that there was at least a possibility of "immortalization" through one's memory.

As to survival in others, Unamuno claimed that it was the prime motor of production and creation. It is, for instance, the basic drive behind sexual love (as Schopenhauer had already pointed out) and, to be sure, behind carnal paternity. Although Unamuno also wrote that "the longing for immortality is nothing but a flower of the longing for descendants," he most often emphasized the primacy of the former over the latter. Human beings aspire to perpetuate themselves, consciously or not, by begetting children who will carry on into the future some of the characteristics of their progenitors. And since the children of the flesh are, according to Unamuno, the prototype of the children of the spirit, it may be said that artists, heroes, and saints pursue the same end as parents: to perpetuate themselves—by means of their works, their deeds, and their actions. Thus, if Don Quixote wishes to be famous "not only in this age, but in the centuries to come," not only throughout La Mancha, but in all Spain and to the ends of the earth, it is because he will not resign himself to perishing. Survival is also, therefore, survival through descendants, through works, and through memory. The problem here is to know whether the works of man will last forever. And as these works, and mankind itself, seem doomed to extinction, we must consider this kind of immortality—in the event it deserves the name—a most unsatisfactory one. Of course, Unamuno acknowledged this, but he proclaimed that, satisfactory or not, this kind of survival—or the hope of it—made it possible for men to go on living without completely despairing. If our lives were confined within too narrow limits, and were not reflected in the mind and in the memory of others, we would probably lose the will to live.

18   The "agony" of Christianity

Although Unamuno looked everywhere for hints of survival and immortality, and welcomed them at the same time that he doubted them, there is every reason to suppose that his thoughts on immortality reached a dramatic climax when he was confronted with the way in which Christian authors treated this same problem. Basically, the decisive motives of which Unamuno availed himself for his concepts and his dreams of eternization, were predominantly Christian. At any rate, whenever he wanted to probe deeply into the question of immortality, he also inquired about the question of the nature and meaning of Christianity. He surveyed the agony of immortality—and of life—and "the agony of Christianity" with the same anguished hope. The Christianity from which Unamuno's thinking on immortality springs is of the conflicting and tragic type. He saw a perpetual contradiction in the heart of Christianity which both tears it apart and revitalizes it. This contradiction reveals itself in a series of conflicts in the course of which the very notion of Christianity perishes only to come alive again with renewed vigor.

One of these conflicts emerges as soon as we try to define Christianity. Unamuno proposed a formula that was strangely reminiscent of the definitions outlined by some German neo-Kantian philosophers: Christianity, he wrote, "is a value of the universal spirit." It would seem that Unamuno abandoned his impassioned vocabulary just as he was about to deal with one of his greatest themes. But when we place his definition in its context we are again on familiar ground. The complete definition reads: "Christianity is a value of the universal spirit with its roots in the intimate core of human individuality." In one single sentence the first contradiction in Christianity is clearly revealed: the contradiction of intemporal values with human experience. As a consequence we have the conflict between the universal and the individual elements, between the so-called "objective spirit" and the radical subjectivity of human life. Perhaps these conflicts might be ironed out by declaring that Christianity as a universal value exists only to the degree that it is rooted in experience. But since Unamuno believed that the reverse was equally true, that the world of experience exists only when encased in objectivity, in values, and in universality, the conflict persists. The personal and the universal components of Christianity coexist in a state of war. Christianity must be true—and hence be universal—and must be experienced—and hence be personal. We cannot do away with one of these elements merely to enhance the other, because then Christianity would lose its *raison d'être*. Christianity, in short, is a series of dogmas *and* a series of personal experiences. The paradox is obvious: one destroys the other, but cannot live without it. Accordingly, there is no "essence of Christianity," and the efforts of German theologians and philosophers to unearth it only exemplify that typically Teutonic intellectual wastefulness. Unamuno's "definition" is not a definition; it is an "invitation" to penetrate the mystery of Christianity. Perhaps, after all, Christianity has no essence; it simply exists, and, as all existences, wrestles with itself.

There are many contradictions and antitheses in Christianity which Unamuno points out. Three of them deserve special attention: the antithesis of Evangelism and Church dogmas; the conflict between the intemporal character of a religious doctrine and the temporal character of life; and the contrast between social and individual Christianity—a contrast similar to, if not the same as, that treated by Kierkegaard under the heading "Christianity versus Christendom." There seems to be little doubt that "Christianity must be defined agonizingly, polemically, by analogy with war." After all, Unamuno reminds his readers, Christ came to earth to bring war, and not peace.

I shall consider for a moment a conflict that was much discussed when Unamuno wrote his book, *The Agony of Christianity*: the conflict between the social and the individual (or rather, personal) components of Christian doctrine. Social Christianity is an attempt to cure the ills and evils of society by reforming it according to Christian norms. These norms are sometimes based on the Gospels, which are supposed to contain in capsule form principles whose application may help to "resolve the socioeconomic problem, that of poverty, of wealth, and the distribution of things in this life." At times they are based on social principles developed by Christian Churches—and in particular by the Catholic Church—in order to cope with the increasingly acute social problems of the modern age; a "just order" is then put forward as the indispensable basis of Christian society. On the other hand, individual (or personal) Christianity proposes to solve no other problem than that of the individual consciousness. This type of Christianity may appear as an ethical attitude or as a purely religious one—this last consisting in an effort to "imitate" Christ. It would seem that personal Christianity is more authentic than social Christianity, and Unamuno certainly began by favoring the former when he declared that Christianity—as social Christianity—"kills Christendom, which is a thing for solitary men." As soon as we focus our attention on the completely "solitary" character of Christianity, however, we notice that Christianity cannot endure; only a society of Christians—and a solidly organized one at that—can perpetuate the Christian attitude. We are thus confronted with a hopeless situation: social Christianity kills Christendom, and Christendom dissolves Christianity. Some would say that there is no need to push the conflict to this extreme, and that a more reasonable course would be to reconcile the personal and the social components of Christianity. But by now it should not be necessary to note that Unamuno would have fiercely denounced this eclecticism as Philistine. Not, therefore, "either one or the other"—and not "one *and* the other"—but "one *against* the other—and *vice versa.*" It is only insofar as Christianity and Christendom embrace in a struggle that the Christian attitude can become a vital one. We have here an example of "the agony of Christianity." Christianity must continually struggle with itself in order to survive.

19   The "agony" of history

"The agony of Christianity" is, in a way, similar to "the agony of history." Unamuno never used this last expression, but there is every reason to suppose that he would have accepted it as an adequate description of his feelings on the nature of "historical reality." For Unamuno history was what remains and what passes away, and most important of all, that insoluble dialectics between the two. Unamuno would agree with those who have viewed history —human history, that is—as meaningless, but he would also agree with those who have considered human history the greatest and the most meaningful of all realities. To be sure, in Unamuno's writings we do not find a fully developed philosophy of history. His thoughts on history are often vague and at times excessively apocalyptic. "History," as "God's train of thought on man's earth," he writes, "has no final human goal, it moves toward oblivion, toward unconsciousness." At the same time he claimed that history was "the only living thing, the eternal present, the fleeting moment that in passing away remains, and in remaining passes away." Furthermore, he occasionally emphasized the importance of tradition—essentially historical—but he also hailed the significance of what he called "the eternal present"—essentially ahistorical and atemporal. All this would seem to indicate that, although human history exists in its own right, it cannot be explained by itself, and needs some reality that transcends it.

These contradictions can be understood in the light of the Unamunian conception of "intrahistory," to which we have already referred and which we shall treat in greater detail later. The essence of human history is for Unamuno what lies within history —the so-called "eternal tradition." Therefore, Unamuno did not maintain that human history must be explained by something extrahistorical—by the unfolding of God's spirit, or by the evolution of nature, to give only two examples. He also rejected the idea of history as a collection of political, social, economic, cultural facts having no other foundation than themselves—even when arranged in a certain order that provides a satisfactorily causal explanation. The notions of "intrahistory" and of "eternal tradition," on the other hand, seemed more promising to him because they gave human history a meaning in terms of itself. Unamuno's views in this connection were probably conditioned by two assumptions: one, that the essence of history is personal in character; and two, that there is always something eternal in the "moment." The first assumption means simply that it is human beings who make history, so that history is, ultimately, the "history of men's souls." The second assumption is intended to mean that although historical events are unique and, as such, cannot be repeated, the eternal in them persists forever. This second assumption is, of course, the more Unamunian of the two and, in a sense, the more original. At any rate, it seems that Unamuno's views—or more exactly, feelings—on history were intimately related to his speculations on the problem of immortality. This is why we have entered them here as a conclusion of our analysis of the problem. Just as Unamuno wanted to pause in each moment, not merely to enjoy it, but rather to make it eternal, he also wanted to see in each one of the events of history a possibility or, at least, a glimpse of that eternity he dreamed of for himself. Thus he could say that to live eternally was to live within history—by no means, therefore, outside of it, in the bosom of God, of Nature, or of some Hegelian Universal Spirit. As so often in his writings, Unamuno does not provide any proof for this contention; instead, he invites us to "feel" the touch of eternity in historical events. Yet this eternity is in no way a pure intemporality: it is an eternity made up of—piled high with—time.

FOUR

Spain – Quixotism

20 *Europeanizers and Hispanizers*

WITH AGONY AND TRAGEDY everywhere, it is no surprise to re-discover them in connection with Spain, Unamuno's permanent obsession. However, Unamuno did not apply his philosophy of tragedy to "the problem of Spain." On the contrary, it was his intuition of the conflictive nature of Spain and of all things Spanish which enabled him to evolve his philosophy of tragedy.

At any rate, we must not think that Unamuno's preoccupation with Spain was the result of a narrow-minded and outmoded nationalism. And this because, first, "Spain" may designate a vast and complex cultural area comprising not only continental Spain but also Portugal, and Spanish and Portuguese America. And second, because although Unamuno was a Spaniard par excellence, he was also a "universal man." An exclusively Spanish point of view would not do justice to Unamuno's ideas on, and ideals for, Spain. His treatment of "the problem of Spain" also included a number of opinions about the relations between Spain and Europe, and others on "the problem of Europe." Thus, unless we are aware of the inclusiveness of Unamuno's concern, we cannot understand his most original contributions to the problems here discussed, nor grasp the meaning of his search for "the eternal Spain" beneath the transient events of Spanish history. As we shall discover, "the eternal Spain" is ultimately an "intravital" and "intrahistoric," not a lifeless and ahistoric, Spain.

Unamuno developed his views on the subject in ever more personal reactions to the long and bitter debate between Europeanizers—those who favored, and wanted "to catch up with," Europe —and the Hispanizers—those who proclaimed that Spaniards needed to maintain their own tradition at all costs; if necessary, against Europe. This debate was particularly lively in the years of Unamuno's youth, and to a great extent conditioned the literary "rediscovery of Spain" by the members of the Generation of 1898. The Europeanizers were goaded to action by their acute discomfort at being obliged to compare the political, social, economic, and intellectual conditions of Spain and Europe. By "Europe" they meant Germany, France, England—sometimes Italy, and occasionally Switzerland and the Scandinavian countries. They meant to prove to all complacent Spaniards that there was a deplorable material and cultural lag in their country, and to warn their compatriots that this lag had increased with the passing years. Europe, they felt, had been making continual progress—political democracy, economic expansion, and scientific creation—whereas Spain had been, at least since the seventeenth century, or perhaps earlier, in a continual decline.

A list of the reasons suggested to explain this decline on Spain's part would fill an entire book. Nevertheless, these reasons can be reduced to seven basic types: (1) psychological reasons—a constitutional incapacity for fulfilling the demands of the modern era, a sharp sense of inferiority coupled with an excessive feeling of pride; (2) religious reasons—dogmatism, the Inquisitional spirit, intolerance; (3) demographic reasons—depopulation caused by continual wars and by the conquest of America; (4) economic reasons—the upset caused by the introduction of the "American gold," the destruction of farming by the Mesta, the crushing of incipient industry by the oppressive regulations of the state, and later, the myopic protectionism offered to a still shaky industry; (5) social reasons—the demise of a promising middle class at Villalar; (6) political reasons—misrule, ineffectual administration, the continued and ineradicable "Philipization" (or, in the words of Ortega y Gasset, "Tibetanization") of Spain; (7) educational reasons—illiteracy, insufficient attention to scientific research and technological ingenuity.

Although it was not always easy to substantiate these reasons (state administration, for instance, was far from being badly organized or ineffectual), this over-all picture seemed close to the truth. And in order to shake off this burdensome heritage, the Europeanizers (Juan Valera in a subdued manner; Joaquín Costa with a roaring voice) proposed to follow the "European" example and introduce a greater amount of religious tolerance, increase political liberties, and reform the social and economic structure. Since it was felt (and is still felt nowadays, although with much less rhetoric and more attention to concrete developments than before) that attention to the European example would provide a solution for many of Spain's ills, an "open door" policy toward Europe—and a corresponding "deafricanization" of Spain—was considered an absolute necessity. Spain must be "regenerated" materially and spiritually (indeed, some of the Europeanizers were called "Regenerationists"). A few even thought that the achievement of this goal would inevitably entail, at least for a transitional period, a certain amount of what the Hispanizers declared to be the greatest of all evils for a country: imitation of foreign ways of life.

The tenets of the Hispanizers were at the other extreme. There were many things, they argued, that were wrong with Spain, but not those with which the Europeanizers concerned themselves.

On the contrary, the chief trouble was that Spain had blindly adopted all the modern European vices: disbelief, skepticism, rationalism, the overevaluation of material rather than spiritual things, of science rather than belief, and of reason rather than faith. Therefore, the solution was a simple one: return to the "authentic tradition" of Spain, which the Europeanizers profaned, and recover the "lost virtues of past epochs." The origin of these "virtues" was sometimes traced to a single primeval source, but more often they were believed to have been molded during certain well-defined historical periods—under the Catholic kings, under Philip II, and during the Counter Reformation. It was not the differences between Europe and Spain which should give cause for alarm, but their increasing similarities. In agreement with the Europeanizers on one point at least, the Hispanizers proclaimed that Spain must be "regenerated," but instead of proceeding with an eye to the future they felt it would be more beneficial to return to the "past."

We have outlined the two extreme positions because they throw light on the background of the debate; but it must also be remembered that a good number of the attitudes toward the problem were infinitely more subtle. Menéndez y Pelayo, for example, although convinced of the need for a resurrection of the "true greatness" of Spain and a recapturing of the "virtues of the past," now obscured by mere imitation and "heterodoxy," suspected that the "spirit of the Enlightenment," responsible for much of Europe's advance, could not be discarded with a single stroke of the pen. On the contrary, the task was to discover to what degree Spain had helped in the formation of this spirit of enlightenment— and thereby, in the creation of science, philosophy, and technology —in many cases anticipating Europe's most highly acknowledged achievements. Spain, Menéndez y Pelayo concluded, need not imitate Europe because it had been, and still was, fundamentally European, although many Spaniards persisted in ignoring the fact.

Did not the "Black Legend" of Spanish "colonization" lose much of its dark hue when the historical truth was examined with a degree of care? Could not much of the cruelty, authoritarianism, and fanaticism thought to be so characteristically Spanish, be found in equal abundance in Europe as well? Hence, one must beware of those who drew an excessively sharp dividing line between Spain and Europe. If there was any difference, Menéndez y Pelayo felt it was due to Europe's having always followed the "straight path," whereas Spain had more often followed a "crooked" one that had caused her to confuse the development of science with the destruction of faith, and the fostering of liberalism with the production of anarchy. The spirit of tolerance must be upheld, though never so as to sanction "error"—anyone who, like Menéndez y Pelayo, considered himself a "hammer of heretics" could not go that far—against stupidity, lack of culture, and bad taste. Juan Valera, on the other hand, felt differently. A Europeanizer with few equals, an enemy of arrogance, disdain, and fanaticism—in which he saw the principal causes of Spain's alienation from modern Europe—he was equally strong in his desire to help make Spain more truly herself. As the critic Guillermo de Torre has noted, this self-styled skeptic would react vehemently whenever any foreigner arrogantly presumed to judge anything Spanish. To rant for the sake of ranting was pernicious, intolerable; one must try to understand, smooth over, rectify. In short, all fanaticism, all exaltation and delirium, all extremes—no matter what faction sponsored them—must be discarded. Only in this way would Spain cease to swim against the European current. Then there was Pérez Galdós' point of view. Firmly convinced that there was much in modern Europe which Spaniards would do well to consider carefully, and seduced by political institutions and social customs best exemplified in the area north of the Pyrenees, and even on the other side of the English Channel, he was at the same time a patient rediscoverer, and a passionate lover of every

corner—human and urban—of Spain. His profound appraisal of
the history and life of his country was almost unequaled; few of
his contemporaries knew how to extract, as he did, the permanent
lessons in the lives and gestures most deeply embedded in the
historical tradition of his country. And finally, let us recall Francisco Giner de los Ríos, who taught students to see and love
Europe, but also to understand Spain, her villages, her people, and
her countryside. Thus, it is apparent that there was an abundance
of intermediate positions of all shades, and that, consequently,
the extremes I have mentioned and the conflict referred to between
Europeanizers and Hispanizers must be taken *cum grano salis.*
This would seem to suggest the conclusion that certain syncopated
rhythms, certain outrageous posturings, certain overly abrupt
modes of action, were the exception in Spanish life, owing, quite
simply, to external pressures or unfortunate lapses.

21   *Spain as a conflict*

The above is a difficult conclusion to accept if one is intent upon
a profound examination of that life, and determined to come up
with all that it contains of value. This conclusion was never
Unamuno's. Does this mean that he considered it more important
to approve one of the extreme attitudes that we began by listing
rather than the other? Some have felt this to be true. They notice
that he not only spoke out for Europeanization and, more often,
for Hispanization, but seemed to jump from one to the other as
well. Accordingly, Unamuno would have been a Europeanizer
when he proposed to "lock the sepulcher of the Cid," shortly before 1897, becoming a diehard Hispanizer when he proclaimed,
both in the *Life of Don Quixote and Sancho* and at the end of

Tragic Sense of Life, that Spain had never followed the "economic" methods of modern Europe: that the only "economy" to which she had been faithful was that "eternal and divine economy" of which the Counter Reformation had been the outstanding historical example; that (like Don Quixote) "Spain was demented"; that there was no need to worry about strengthening democratic institutions, producing technological wonders or inventing abstruse philosophical systems (for, he said, if it was a question of inventing, "let Europe do that!"); and, finally, that it was useless to be annoyed by a Europe that was nothing but a "shibboleth"—a deception, a mirage, a fetish. On superficial evidence, therefore, Unamuno seemed to be not just one Hispanizer among many, but the most outspoken of them all. Going to the other extreme, he seemed to have become (as Ortega y Gasset so bitterly complained) a staunch defender of "Africanism," a standard-bearer of "barbarianism." And it is perfectly true that for a while Unamuno shunned all moderation, so much so that the traditionalism of the Hispanizers seemed tainted with "modernism" when contrasted with his own.

We must not, however, read Unamuno too literally, nor forget that he sincerely enjoyed reducing doctrines to absurdity by wrapping them in startling paradoxes. We recognize that Unamuno's frequently brash exclamations lend weight to the idea that he became an uncompromising "Hispanizer." But this idea is in conflict with all that we know of him. Unamuno would find little satisfaction in a conventional traditionalism, which he always judged vain, pompous, and shallow. And since, finally, it would be embarrassing to admit that he could have felt any profound sympathy for any one of the moderate (and, he would probably say, "hybrid") attitudes of which we have given some examples, it will be necessary to strike out in a new direction, in order to discover what Unamuno really felt about Spain—and in what way this feeling can be dove-tailed into the permanent structure of his thought.

The term *'adentramiento'* ('inner-directing', literally), already examined with another purpose in mind, provides an illuminating indication in this respect. It would seem, at first, to suggest a retreat—quite appropriate in view of Spain's having suffered innumerable setbacks in the course of her history. Having failed so many times—or, rather, having never realized all of her over-ambitious projects—she would be foolish to try once more for success. There were, then, two alternatives: to adopt a policy adjusted to her means and to her diminished power; or to direct her efforts inward and initiate an untiring self-exploration. The first course of action is the business of statesmen; the second one, the task of poets and thinkers. This was the substance of Ganivet's "thesis." To a degree it was also the "thesis" of Unamuno. But he was less concerned than Ganivet with an "agonizing reappraisal" in the field of political action; he emphasized the spiritual side of inner-direction. Now, the motion described by the term *'adentramiento'* must not be considered a retrograde one. Ganivet proclaimed that a "withdrawal toward the self" (*"retirarse hacia sí"*) did not necessarily imply a lessening of the force and vigor of national life. Unamuno was even more outspoken on this point. After all, solitude had never seemed to him more than a preliminary step in the search for companionship. "Only loneliness," he wrote, "can melt away this thick layer of shame that isolates us one from another; only in loneliness can we find ourselves; and when we do so, we discover we are all brothers in loneliness. And if we are unable to love each other, it is only because we are unable to remain alone." Therefore, once we reach the man within we are able to act out what we have already seen to be one of Unamuno's major obsessions: to flow, to abound, to pour out. Only well water is contained; spring water always overflows. Here also, "draw in in order to expand" (*"concentrarse para irradiar"*) was deemed by him the only fruitful norm, and it was precisely this injunction that neither "Europeanizers" nor "Hispanizers," "progressives" nor "traditionalists" were able to follow. Won by outward appearances—or by false essentials—they all neglected to notice that the salvation of a country can come only from the heart of the country itself, and that only by plunging down into its own "vital dwelling place" (*"morada vital"*)—to use a term whose meaning Américo Castro has so thoroughly explored—could a country touch solid bottom and move forward again without weakening or falsifying its existence.

But moving forward again did not mean reviving past glories or building up political and military power. Unamuno's point of view must not be confused with that of the traditionalists. The defenders of a so-called glorious tradition were, in fact, prisoners of a quite limited tradition, for instead of breathing life into the community they managed to retard, paralyze, swamp, and, finally, ruin it. Traditionalists were as blind to the real powers of a human community as the "progressives." "Progressives" were so haunted by the future that eventually they could only dream of utopias. The traditionalists were haunted by the past and inevitably became reactionaries. Despite their claims to the contrary, both were concerned exclusively with dreams, and not with that real fountain of spiritual power which always can be heard by anyone who is able to decipher its hidden harmonies.

Thus it was natural that Unamuno should have resolutely struggled against that variety of shallow patriotism which consisted of coddling the "stubble and chaff"; natural that he should have proclaimed the need to escape "that great pagan subject": history. History was to Unamuno essentially "the history of death"; Spaniards must therefore do all they could in order to rid themselves of that "damnable history that oppressed and suffocated" them. The Spain for which Unamuno searched was "not of this world"; it was to be found, as he wrote in one of his poems, "in the depths of the blue above it." He thus proposed the idea of an "eternal and celestial Spain"—with equal justification we could say "the idea of an eternal and subterranean Spain"—which scandalized traditionalists and progressives alike.

Let us not misinterpret Unamuno's impassioned vocabulary. This "eternal Spain" is not a pure Platonic idea transcending all tangible realities. Nor is it the dream of a megalomaniac—a thing of splendor and grandeur which reflects only ridicule on the dreamer. Unamuno has said that his "eternal Spain" was not extratemporal, but intratemporal, nor extrahistoric, but intrahistoric. He also wrote that we must plunge into "the eternal tradition, the mother of the ideal, which is nothing but tradition itself projected into the future." With these cryptic words he expressed as well as he could the intuition that Spain's authentic being was to be found above and beyond the petty attractions of glory and power, whether past or future. The true life of Spain was to be found in the hearts of the Spaniards themselves if they could only do away with historical tradition and the fallacies of traditionalism and progressivism, and direct their exploration inward to the core of the innermost self and there discover the permanent substructure underlying all historical events. For history, past or future, was the outer covering of the soul's purely internal rhythm.

Needless to say, the innermost self of a human community does not live in quiet and peace; like all else, it thrives on conflict —and conflict with itself. "Spanish existence consists of a polemic," Américo Castro has written in a quite Unamunian vein. A polemic in which Europeanizers and Hispanizers, progressives and traditionalists take part—and this is their justification; even the "extremists" and the "moderates" can be said to participate in the conflict. There may be "two Spains," but they are united; not by intellectual compromise, but in a vital dialectic. Like the man of flesh and blood, Spain lives in order to "forge itself a soul," and this even when its history proves to be only a process of self-destruction (*"desvivirse"*).

"Like the man of flesh and blood"—this means that Unamuno

believes he can discern the precise substance of the human being in the innermost core of what seems to be only a particular "national community." This is the meaning of Unamuno's injunction: "Let us Hispanize Europe!"—a step toward a "Hispanization of the world." This "Hispanization" does not entail any political or ideological imposition, or any kind of influence or domination— things of a "rotten past." It means simply a "display" of what may be called "the humanity of man." This is why Unamuno's pre-occupation with Spain had little, if anything, to do with nationalism or patriotism. It was not a question of marking time in that "enraged or doleful replevin" which, according to the Argentine writer Jorge Luis Borges, was the single, monotonous entertainment of too many Spanish writers of the nineteenth century. Nor was it a question of dreaming, more or less lazily, of a hypothetical and future magnificence. Unamuno was very clear on this point: if Spaniards—and, in general, all human beings—wanted to fulfill themselves, they must remove the crust of the past, and avoid the mirage of the future. They must not live according to tradition, or according to reason, or according to tradition corrected by reason, or even reason seconded by tradition. Their life must be based on their own powers, on their own possibilities. Once they learned to disregard what *others* wanted them to be, they must strive to be what *they themselves* wanted to be.

It will be argued that all this is vague (or metaphorical), and that the much-praised "intrahistory" is either history itself reduced to a few essentials, or means nothing at all. This objection is reasonable. But we must be careful not to miss the important point in this Unamunian intuition: that in all history there is much that is alien to the "internal life" of a community and much that might very well "not have happened" without basically modifying this life. Behind this intuition was the idea that the values, toward the achievement of which human existence is directed, can help us to a better understanding of that human existence than even history itself. In fact, Unamuno's ideas on history may serve in any attempt to understand life, whether it be human existence in general, or certain features of Spanish life.

"Spanish life" is thus a symbol of "human existence," but it is more easily detected in all those communities that participate directly in the Spanish tradition: the Hispano-Portuguese, the Hispano-American, and the Ibero-American. With the "Portuguese brothers," Unamuno included the South American and the "Ibero-American brothers" in his speculations about the Spanish soul. On the surface, Unamuno's phraseology appears to be another example of the outmoded political rhetoric that some Spanish statesmen still use in toasts at Columbus Day banquets, but it is really the result of a vital, constant interest in the ways of life and feeling particular to Spanish and Ibero-Americans. Unlike those who ignored the existence of Spanish and Portuguese America, or those who considered them little more than an intellectual colony, Unamuno took them into his heart, even though at times he lectured them very severely. He believed that Americans of Spanish and Portuguese descent lived exactly as did their European counterparts, even when they fought the latter for political or intellectual independence. Their life, he felt, was a polemic; they too felt the heartbeat of their intrahistory beneath the crust of historical events; and, finally, they too sensed that they were a symbol of "pure humanity."

22   The Quixotic soul

Let us also add: sensed that they were the symbol of pure Quixotism; for the Spanish spirit, the human spirit, and the Quixotic spirit were but three manifestations of the same reality according to Unamuno. His "philosophy of Quixotism" is as much an essential ingredient of his philosophy of the Spanish soul, as the latter is of his philosophy of human existence. Unamuno worshiped Don Quixote, and often took Cervantes to task for failing to understand his own hero. Unamuno's weakness for the use of paradox was never more evident than in his speculations on the nature and meaning of "Quixotism." He considered Don Quixote and Sancho men of flesh and blood, more real than Cervantes himself. He made a "religion" of Quixotism. He considered it the natural one for Spaniards and, for that matter, for all human beings who were guided by ideals. He proposed a "crusade" to rescue Don Quixote from the hands of those who saw nothing in Cervantes' work but a "literary masterpiece." There is no need to take this proposal of Unamuno's too literally, but the fireworks of his paradoxes must not keep us from recognizing his serious attempt to describe the nature of the "Spanish soul" and the soul of all mankind. At the heart of this soul is the longing for that immortality that Unamuno considered the trademark of humanity.

Like the "Spanish soul," the "Quixote soul" does not exhaust its capacity for activity by going out into the world to make history. To be sure, Quixotic deeds took place in history—they were located in a definite geographical area and permeated by the customs and ideals of a certain historical age—but they were always nourished by that profound "dream" that pulsated beneath all historical and circumstantial events. "The adventures of our knight," Unamuno wrote, "flower in time and on earth, but their roots are in eternity." As a symbol of what Spain and the Spanish community on both sides of the Atlantic offered the world, Don Quixote possessed "a soul," and only by taking it into consideration could his deeds be properly understood and adequately evaluated. The Cervantes scholars wrongly assumed that the significance of *Don Quijote* was in what the hero said, or in the way in which he said it. They were unable to see that the only really interesting point was what Cervantes' hero longed to be. Not, of course, because Don Quixote was an incarnation *avant la lettre* of the modern "Faustian spirit," for whom actions were more important than words and deeds. The "Faustian spirit"—as described by Goethe in one of Faust's monologues—is, at bottom, an example of the philosophy of "pure Will," entailing a directionless dynamism. Quixotism, on the other hand, is an example of a will directed toward the performance of the good; an example of an impulse destined to make this good available to all human beings. The philosophy of Quixotism has, therefore, little or nothing to do with the philosophies proposed by either traditionalists or progressives. Traditionalists dream of the false glories of the past; progressives preach the use of "the regenerative decoction, the customhouse poultice, the hydraulic blister plaster." These last solutions—some of which (the least ideological and the most concrete) are still quite vital for Spaniards today—seemed mere abstractions to Unamuno, mere blueprints and programs which amounted to nothing when set beside that supreme reality: the forging of personality—of a "soul of bulk and substance." Don Quixote symbolizes the quest for personality as opposed to the emphasis on fact and ideas. To his fellow men he seems a lunatic, but he is a symbol of "pure spiritual maturity"—an expression that Unamuno, probably on purpose, left undefined. This is why Don Quixote is an enemy of caution; he puts his whole self into every action. But the action he undertakes has a purpose and, basically, it is suffused with prudence. Cervantes frequently uses the term "unreason" (*"sinrazón"*) as a description of Quixotic madness; and Unamuno maintained that, far from being a lack of reason, "unreason" was a variety of "superreason." It was a reason proper to ideals and not merely to ideas.

The "Holy Crusade" that Unamuno undertook in order to ransom the tomb of that "Knight of Madness," Don Quixote, was a first step in the search for a "pure spiritual maturity." Accordingly, it was necessary to free Don Quixote from the tomb where the "Knights of Reason"—the rationalists, the worshipers of common sense, the men who acted according to well-defined programs —have him chained—and perhaps embalmed. The "Knights of Reason" pretend to follow the dictates of ideas, but are, in fact, unable to sacrifice their lives for an idea. They are "incapable of marrying a great and pure idea, and begetting children by it"; instead, they "live in concubinage with ideas." They do not understand that ideas must be taken—or rather, embraced—as ideals. On this point Unamuno seemed to be reworking the Socratic attitude that an idea is worthless unless one is willing to commit one's self to it, to live by, and die for it. Being less of a rationalist than Socrates, however, Unamuno did not attempt to define ideas; it was enough for him that he "felt" them. And he felt them as ideals, for only as ideals could they become the essential ingredients of human life.

The Cervantes scholars, Unamuno thought, failed to grasp the meaning of the Quixotic attitude. To begin with, they paid too much attention to Don Quixote's reasoning, to his knowledge of the Italian language, to his discourse on arms and letters. They treated him as a character in a novel and not as a man of flesh and blood. And if they noticed the Quixotic ideals, they were unable to see that Don Quixote's deeds were always purposeful. As a matter of fact, the deeds had a double purpose, in part ethical: Don Quixote—and also Sancho, his "other half"—constantly strives to become good—"pure good, uncomplicated by theological subtleties, good and nothing but good"; in part, divine: Don Quixote constantly strives to become immortal. The Quixotic defense of ideals is not, therefore, a defense of *just any* ideals, but only those of goodness and eternity.

Don Quixote's striving for immortality manifests itself in a way that at first seems mere self-worship: as the desire for glory and renown. But this egotism is only apparent. It is really the expression of a longing not to die. This is, according to Unamuno, the "innermost core, the core of all the cores of Quixotic madness." Like all human beings who have not been enslaved by things, Don Quixote shows that he can believe (while doubting) in "the impossible." But since man cannot continue to live—as man—without attempting "the impossible," Don Quixote's madness is a sublime expression of sanity, paradoxical as this may seem at first. Don Quixote's madness is thus more sane than the sanity of others, to use the terms employed by Saint Paul in speaking of God. This madness touches common sense, because it is an exaltation of that "personal sense" that Unamuno identifies with the "human sense."

There is little doubt that Unamuno goes too far. There is too much talk of madness in his philosophy of Quixotism. He seems too easily mastered by a desire to *épater le bourgeois*. But, after all, he belonged (as Ortega y Gasset noted) to the same literary generation as Bernard Shaw—a generation that made paradox the norm of expression. Nevertheless, beneath Unamuno's puns and paradoxes lies a sincere desire to remind men of their human condition, to bring into focus the realization that they are mortal and at the same time desire to become immortal. The philosophy of Quixotism is a basic ingredient in Unamuno's philosophy of the "man of flesh and blood." Unamuno wants us to become as real as Don Quixote, because the ultimate reality of man is determined by what each man wants to be.

It is not enough, however, to ransom Don Quixote. We must ransom Sancho too, because, according to Unamuno, his faith is even more admirable than his master's, because it is more beset by doubt. Unamuno declared that Sancho was "an indissoluble half of Don Quixote." The conventional view of the idealism of the master and the realism—one might say, materialism—of the servant, does not observe that as Cervantes' book unfolds Sancho gradually becomes Quixotic. To be sure, he becomes so unconsciously, and never claims to be more than his master's shadow.

But by the end of the book he proves that he has completely assimilated Don Quixote's spirit, and that his Quixotism is even more pure than his master's. In the final analysis it is Don Quixote who has corrupted the purity of his own faith through an excessive pride in his self-confidence, whereas Sancho, so full of common sense and so timid in his courage, never once jeopardizes the true Quixotic faith. Sancho's faith is of the right kind; it is not faith in himself, but in his master—who seems to him to be the incarnation of an idea. Don Quixote sees giants where there are only windmills; his mettle and his desire for justice are often simply the result of a feverish imagination. Sancho, on the other hand, sees the windmills as windmills, and yet does not falter in his faith. And finally, Sancho's faith is a truly Unamunian one, for it is nourished by doubt. He does not believe that the barber's basin (*"bacía"*) is Mambrino's helmet (*"yelmo"*), nor does he think that it is only a basin, but a combination of both, a "basin-helmet" (*"baciyelmo"*). And when at the end of his career, Don Quixote betrays his faith, and decides to renounce adventuring, Sancho implores him to return to the highroads of La Mancha in the pursuit of ideal justice. Unamuno is therefore able to conclude that although Don Quixote may die, Sancho never will. He is the true "inheritor of Don Quixote's spirit," and perhaps the very essence of Quixotism.

Unamuno's philosophy of Quixotism was at first a corollary of his philosophy of the Spanish soul, an illustration of it. But although Unamuno was not a systematic thinker in the conventional—or rather, academic—sense of the word, he was extremely consistent, and even repetitious in the development of his favorite themes. Small wonder, then, that his commentaries on the life of Cervantes' hero are interwoven with the themes we have already examined: the problem of the man of flesh and blood, the idea of tragedy, the longing for immortality, and so on. Now, if the name of any philosophical discipline were needed for Unamuno's thoughts on Don Quixote, "ethics" would be the least inappropriate. For Unamuno, Don Quixote is the symbol of a moral ideal, and although Unamuno would certainly resist any attempt to label him, his ethics would be best described as an existential ethics of value. This ethics is not based upon nature, or upon history, and certainly not on a Platonic realm of eternal ideas. It has its roots in the depths of each human being, and yet transcends personality in the sense that any person who behaved as Unamuno proposed must aim at goals that no mortal could ever reach. Thus, in the ethics, as in everything else, conflict is master. Ortega y Gasset's teacher, the neo-Kantian philosopher Hermann Cohen, was not far from the truth when he saw in Don Quixote's deeds and words an instance of Fichte's ethics of infinite effort. Unamuno would have shuddered at the thought that what I have called his ethics resembled Fichte's, or any other philosopher's, for that matter. Nevertheless, they have a common source: both spring from the desire to make personality the dynamic center of a conflicting world. If there is any difference between them, it is that whereas for Fichte the only goal of the human consciousness was that of realizing itself, for Unamuno there were two goals— goodness and immortality. And only in the pursuit of these two goals did man have a chance of becoming himself.

FIVE

The Idea of the Word

23 The power of words

UNAMUNO occupied a post—that of professor—and exercised a
profession—that of philologist; yet neither of these activities was
ever the axis of his life; nor were they, on the other hand, mere
accidents. The post was, in the vocabulary, at once administrative
and "metaphysical," of the Spanish Government, a "destiny"
(*destino*): the chair of Greek at the University of Salamanca—
and later, in addition, another of the history of the Spanish
language. Unamuno felt that the profession he exercised entailed
a "mission": to educate people—and not only students—in the
use and misuse of words. Together the two chairs provided
Unamuno with what he needed most: a rostrum. Not just a chair
at the university, and not simply a speaker's platform or pulpit;
but rather, an eminence from which to make his powerful and
resounding voice heard, the voice that was never silent because its
owner never felt that he had said all he should say. I have used the
terms "destiny" and "mission"; I might add that Unamuno con-

sidered his teaching the consequence of a "call," an "existential" as well as, if not more than, an ethical call.

If Unamuno was, as the French critic Jean Cassou has characterized him, "the professor who above all professed a violent dislike of professors," he was also the professor par excellence, for he made all Spain his classroom. There had been professors of this kind before in Spain (Francisco Giner de los Ríos, for one); but none performed this activity more intensely and passionately than Unamuno. Furthermore, Unamuno distinguished himself from all other "professors on a national scale" in that he expressed the wish not only to educate his countrymen, but also, and above all, to stir their souls. Toward this end he often angered them, but he sincerely believed that this was the only way to awaken them, that is, to renew them.

The instrument of this stirring, this awakening and renewal of souls was the word—the spoken and written word. In these words—words of exhortation, of injunction, of indignation—each man could discover what he unknowingly and even intentionally concealed from himself. The "word" was, as it has always been in crucial times, the instrument of revelation—of "personal revelation." For even when Unamuno's words were aimed at a group, a mass, or a community, they had no public or social character, but always a personal one. Through speeches, monologues, and dialogues Unamuno sought to incite souls and transfigure minds. From the very first *Essays* (*Ensayos*), Unamuno championed the cry of "Inward!" against, and instead of, that of "Forward!" "Forward!" was a word of command; "Inward!" a call to renovation. "Forward!" is shouted by those who wish to impose their will; "Inward!" is used by those who struggle to induce a change. The cry of "Forward!" orders one to march shoulder to shoulder with others; that of "Inward!" to stroll "soul to soul" with them. Unamuno would allow only the latter, and he often surmised that one banded together with others only after a previous exasperation with solitude.

If to Unamuno being a professor and a philologist meant more than exercising a profession, this was because both activities allowed him to probe deeply what he considered "the mystery of the word." We say "mystery" because just when we are about to seize its nature, the word eludes us. The "word" cannot be analyzed, Unamuno felt, into meanings or sounds because it is a living, palpitating entity that, like the soul—and for analogous reasons—partakes of matter when most completely immersed in the spirit, and is composed of soul when it seems most nearly reduced to matter—sound waves or splotches of ink. The "word" was, for Unamuno

> blood of the spirit
> and voice that does not diminish
> for all that it fills both worlds.

In view of this, we are almost led to conclude that, in the fashion of that Supreme One described by mystics and Neoplatonists, the word—or the Word—flows forever and spreads without diminishing. Unlike that One, however, the word in Unamuno's sense has body and bulk since it is capable, not only of expressing the truth, but also—and more importantly—of living it. Words are experienced just as joy and sorrow are experienced; words seduce us, exasperate us, move and paralyze us. Words push against the flesh of our souls; we can destroy or convert, lose or save ourselves with words.

For Unamuno, the task of the philologist—the "true" philologist—was not merely that of chasing words in order to pluck out their meaning, structure, or relationships; it was to enter into them in order to live—or die—with them. If Unamuno combated and despised the professional philologists, the "exhumers" of words

or traditions, it was because he wished to be a philologist by vocation, that is, a philosopher. For him, a philosopher was a man
capable of raising the myriad possibilities of human speech to their
highest power, capable of unearthing and developing the secular
metaphors of his own language to the greatest possible extent. This
was what Plato had done: expressed the philosophical possibilities
of the Greek language. Here it would seem that Unamuno shared
the doctrine of many contemporary thinkers, that the central problem of all philosophy is language itself. Shall we call Unamuno,
the apparent "existentialist," an "analytical philosopher," obsessed
with philosophy as "the analysis of language"? Only if we overlook that Unamuno's equation of philosophy and philology had
little or nothing to do with the linguistic investigations of contemporary logicians and semanticians, and could only remotely be
connected with the philosophical caprices of the grammarians.
Neither one nor the other would admit that the word can be "the
flesh of concepts," or, if they did, they would immediately apolo-
gize for indulging in metaphor or, what would be worse for them,
in passion. Unamuno, however, would not give ground: words were
like other realities, and in particular like human beings; they lived
in a constant state of war, of tension, of conflict. To begin with,
they battle with the concepts from which they are inseparable.
Words cannot live without concepts, but concepts kill words. The
concept is the death that awaits the word, but the word cannot live
without the agony with which the presence of the concept provides
it. The name, "the flesh of concepts," gives words a richer existence, but at the same time stains them with "the taint of original
sin."

24 Words and facts

Through words—living, or rather agonizing words—we know, and consequently, according to the biblical connotation, we beget. Thus words constitute the foundation of that truly decisive act: the creative—or poetic—act. This act has many forms, and literature is but one of them. Strictly speaking, the authentic, creative word transcends all "literature"—which is always something consummated and, therefore, dead. For if living words cannot be reduced to concepts, neither can they be compared to signs. Concepts and signs are only manifestations of the voice, that viva voce that makes itself heard primarily in the dialogue. A dialogue with others or—and for Unamuno it is the same thing— a dialogue with one's self: a monodialogue and, as he said, an autodialogue, in the course of which, he who carries on a dialogue with himself becomes two, three—an entire community. An autodialogue, or monodialogue, is more vivifying than a monologue, or than even a dialogue; for instead of using concepts—which, as a rule, are dogmatic—we then use the live voices of words—which are always "agonizing" and polemical. Polemical and not only dialectical, for the dialectic is, formally, a closed and preordained system of concepts, whereas the polemic is an open, unpredictable discourse. Words are alive only when we do not know what direction they are going to take.

Being "a man of contradictions"—another way of saying "a man of flesh and blood"—means being precisely one of those who, although apparently engaged in a monologue, actually carries on a dialogue, that is, one of those persons who eschews all dogma and all catechism. Living, creative words must express themselves

incessantly in dialogue—or rather in autodialogue—since otherwise they would become a dead artifact, comparable to a dogma
that admits of no doubt or to a faith that never falters. All this
explains, by the way, why Unamuno fought so strenuously against
all forms of scientism. Scientism is, in fact, the dead letter of
science just as mere literature is the dead letter of poetry. True,
living, creative science has little, if anything, to do with scientism.
Such a science admits of self-doubt and can thereby constantly
purge itself of its own poisons. In the same way, true, living,
creative literature is never a purely literary affair; it erases its
own conventional contours and is thus able to renew itself over
and over again. Scientism and mere literature do nothing but
catalogue the universe; science and poetry re-present it and, to a
great extent, in so doing, create it. Now although Unamuno was
a good deal less "antiscientific" than is generally supposed, he
tended to allot an ever greater degree of preëminence to that creative activity par excellence, which he identified with poetry. Real
poetry reveals itself by means of the living word; for this reason,
in opposition to the Faustian principle that in the beginning was
the Action, Unamuno maintained that in the beginning was the
Word. The Word was the "true fact" that he upheld against those
half-facts, and half-truths, concepts and signs. The pseudofacts
hailed by scientism and by literary realism, which one of Unamuno's
characters, Fulgencio, in *Love and Pedagogy* (*Amor y pedagogía*),
called "dilapidated common sense," would immediately fade away
when confronted with the real facts, the real words. If facts are
creative, it is only because words beget them; that is, give them
meaning. The true—*verum*—is, therefore, not the fact itself—
factum—nor even the good—*bonum*—but the spoken—*dictum*.
Verum and *dictum* are the only "transcendentals" between which
a conversion—an ontological conversion—is possible.

25   Words and literature

No wonder Unamuno preferred to see his "literary output" as a poetic and creative endeavor that *had* to use signs and concepts. We may even assume that Unamuno wrote books and articles in such staggering numbers, only because it was physically impossible to speak in person with each one of his fellow humans. If it had proved feasible to sustain a dialogue, viva voce, with each and all at the same time, perhaps Unamuno, in this respect a faithful image of the *homo hispanicus,* would not have written a single line. Literary writing is, to a certain extent, "falsification," in the minds of many Spaniards; doomed by its very nature to be for the most part impersonal, such writing soon becomes conventional and artificial. And what is true of the written word is true of all other forms of communication whose vital source has dried up. The contemporary tendency to reproduce the word by means of the tape recorder would have been a diabolical one to Unamuno, for nothing would have been more distasteful to him than to kill the supreme form of communication: live talk.

Whenever Unamuno's "literature" is an object of criticism, it must always be kept in mind that a poetic *élan* breathes within it, that the written word is meant to be only a shadow of the creative voice. As Rubén Darío noted, Unamuno was first and foremost a poet; and a poet is quite unlike, perhaps even the opposite of, an *homme de lettres.* To be sure, true poetry can wear any guise. Poetry is also, and sometimes superlatively so, novel, essay, legend, and even philosophical treatise. It is significant that, when he spoke of the possible expressions of a feeling—and not just a conception—of the universe, Unamuno should declare that such a feeling "is better mirrored in a poem, in prose or in verse, in a legend, in a novel, than in a philosophical system or in a realistic novel." "And among the great novels (or epic poems, it is all the same)," he added, "along with the *Iliad* and the *Odyssey,* the *Divine Comedy* and *Don Quijote,* and *Paradise Lost* and *Faust,* I count the *Ethics* of Spinoza, Kant's *Critique of Pure Reason,* Hegel's *Logic,* the *Histories* of Thucydides and Tacitus, and of other great historian-poets, and, of course, the *Gospels* of the life of Christ." Such pronouncements would be baffling, if not meaningless, had Unamuno not previously stretched the meaning of "poetry" and enunciated the identification between creative and poetic elements. For unlike the philosophical *system* and the *realistic* novel, the poem creates the things themselves as it expresses them, because instead of merely going around them or simply sketching their outlines, it aspires to penetrate their "souls." Poetry is the soul of things. This soul is unearthed, and also enacted, by the poet; the poet gives things their souls and at the same time shapes his own soul through them. Thus poetry is a kind of fusion of man and things, an objectification of man as well as a subjectification of reality.

Unamuno's entire "literary opus," and for that matter any "literary opus" that is something more than "pure (damned) literature," is, therefore, poetry, whether cast in verse form or in prose, novel or essay, speech or drama. Unamuno never admitted that literature—as poetry—could be classified and pigeonholed in literary "genres"; such "genres" were to him as abstract and bloodless as the categories of Hegel's system were to Bradley. Unamuno's opposition to a classification of literature by literary "genres" gives us a clue to why he invented names in order to describe some "genres" that had only one instance to prove their existence. He used such names as '*Nivola*' (instead of '*novela*'), '*opopeya*' (instead of '*epopeya*'), '*trigedia*' (instead of '*trage-*

dia'). But if he indulged in such fancies it was not because he wanted to add new literary "genres" to the established ones; it was rather because he wished to render absurd the doctrine of literary "genres." Since there are no literary "genres," we can easily admit an infinite number of them—at least one for each poetic work worthy of the name. In the end Unamuno wanted to dissolve all "genres," all classifications, to fuse all "genres" together in the deathless fountain of poetry. For Unamuno the only "literary form" was the poem, and the numerous, perhaps infinite, forms that the poem adopts. Thus we may conjecture that he might even have been willing to compose a "logic," as long as it remained in contact with this primordial fountain— "poetry," the only possible form for him of verbal creation.

26 Words and life

Must we assume, then, that among the diverse forms of expression adopted by Unamuno there is no appreciable difference? That would be a rendering *ad pedem litterae* of what must be understood "according to the spirit" in which it was intended. In accord with the latter, we may say that in Unamuno's "single poem" there are very different "accents" and that the specific quality of each of these lends its character to what we habitually call "poetry," "tragedy," "novel," "speech," "tale," "newspaper article," and "essay." Each of these "genres" possesses its own originality, but this was constituted, as Unamuno had already pointed out with respect to thought, by the accent and the tone rather than determined by the contents or the form. The Unamunian dissolution of the usual literary "genres" no longer seems to be an irritating paradox; it is the affirmation and confirmation of a creative will by which, as Victor Goti remarks in *Mist* (*Niebla*) (Unamuno's *"nivola"*), a thing receives a new name, and is thereby given whatever laws the inventor pleases. Unless we forget this admonition we will again fall victim to that "realism" that is, as Unamuno declared, "a purely external, shadowy, cortical, and anecdotal thing," something that "refers to literary art and not to poetic or creative art." We feel, however, that Unamuno's struggle against realism leaves what might be called "poetic realism" unscathed; with it an authentic reality, an intimate reality and not a written or merely literary one, is created. "A poet," Unamuno wrote in the most celebrated of his poetic credos, "does not draw his creatures—living creatures—according to the methods of realism. The characters created by the realists are usually clothed manikins who move when their strings are pulled, and who carry within them a phonograph that repeats the phrases their puppeteer has collected in the streets and town squares and has jotted down in his book." True reality is foreign to ordinary realism; only authentic or poetic realism can capture it. The realistic writer copies—or rather, pretends to copy—reality and, in so doing, falsifies it. The authentically realistic poet refuses to reproduce, merely, what is, but only because he is aware that "being" is merely a part of reality. As we have seen, anything real is made not only of being, but also of the will to be.

In the next chapter I shall give a more elaborate account of Unamuno's conception of "authentic realism." Here it will suffice to note that the creative will (or urge) of which he spoke so often seems to be an image of chaos and disorder. As a consequence, Unamuno's battle against convention may easily lead to confusion. I suspect, however, that he was aware of this danger, for he implied that to lack a plan was not necessarily to succumb to whim and caprice. The plan of a literary work can be compared to the plan of a human life. Such a plan is progressively conceived as the work is produced. Many rules and directions are laid down in the course of the creative process. As Unamuno wrote, "a plan is not made for life, but rather life traces its plan by being lived." Now, just as with human life, the plan of a literary work consists in not having one, but in being itself its own plan. A plan is not a blueprint, a design, or a scheme; it is at most a project of which we are aware only when it is carried out. If any previously established plan can be detected, in life or in literature, it is only the plan of never reaching an end.

To leave everything unfinished, whether a literary work or life itself, was one of Unamuno's constant aims. Small wonder that his works impress us as being a kind of continuous creation, a sort of "interminable poem." Unamuno often expressed a feeling of distaste, and even horror, at anything that was too "finished," too "perfect," at anything that could not be continued. At one with some Greek philosophers, he thought that "to be finished" and "to be perfect" were basically the same thing; but contrary to these philosophers he dismissed the idea of perfection as being contrary to all sincerity and authenticity. He showed a definite dislike for any form of writing in which there were beautifully autonomous units, as if nothing could be added to them or subtracted from them. He rejected that "mere perfection" of verse and prose whose hallmark is completeness. He constantly hailed those writings that were full of "loose ends," that could be taken up again at any moment, to which one could always return. And so Unamuno's works give the impression that they might be continued indefinitely. There are everywhere "loose ends" offered to the reader as an incitement to dialogue, to polemic, to controversy. Unamuno's writings have always a "dramatic form." And this is not surprising, since they are not intended to be writings at all. They are meant to be the sounds of a human voice.

In the essentially unfinished character of Unamuno's works we encounter once again that impulse to overturn, to pour out, to overflow, of which I have spoken on several occasions, and which so faithfully represents Unamuno's temperament, his aims. Such an impulse is present even when, as in poetic forms fixed by tradition—like the sonnet—all would seem to end with the final verse. But if the last line of any of Unamuno's sonnets is a formal conclusion, it is also a new beginning; the poet has ceased to move his pen, but he keeps his spirit—and the spirit of his readers —mobile. Thus in the majority of cases—as in *Teresa,* in *The Christ of Velázquez* (*El Cristo de Velázquez*), in considerable portions of the *Book of Songs* (*Cancionero*)—Unamuno unequivocally adopts those poetic forms that are least encumbered by formal exigencies and abound with "loose ends" that can be resumed at any time—and developed indefinitely. Not that Unamuno avoids rhythm; on the contrary, he finds it everywhere, even in Kant's *Critiques!* But this rhythm is the rhythm of life. It is not difficult to find hendecasyllables in the *Tragic Sense of Life.* But they are not intended as poetic ornament; they are meant to be songs. Perhaps, after all, Unamuno's writings are songs of a sort, sung by a soul made of living words.

Unamuno was not a spectator, like Ortega y Gasset, nor a preceptor, like Eugenio d'Ors, but as Ernst Robert Curtius has written, an "exciter": *excitator* and not *praeceptor* or *spectator Hispaniae.* In all his writings, he set himself the task of performing—without ever finishing—what he considered the fundamental mission of the "human word": to excite, to disturb, to stir up souls, that he might better entreat them to awaken from their momentary dream and immerse themselves in a more substantial and lasting dream—that of the eternal. To excite, was to shake souls and not simply or not only to "agitate" them (as demagogues usually do). This is, of course, another way of saying: to change, to transform, and ultimately, to transfigure souls. Furthermore, he felt that he must excite them individually, since "nothing has any use or value except what springs from the concrete life itself," and is directed toward the concrete life. The "loose ends" that we find in the works of Unamuno are tossed overboard for the salvation—human salvation—of his fellow men and also, equally, in order to see if man can also live in hope, even when rocked by despair. "They say that to define and to separate is Hellenic; my way is to make indefinite and to confuse." But here to confuse means to drown everything in the original fountainhead of creation and of poetry, to dissolve everything in order to begin a new life and a new dream, cleansed anew and purified. Only in this way can what one *is* coincide with what one *wants to be*. We may conclude that only in this way can utopia embrace reality.

SIX

The Idea of Fiction

27 *The "personal" novel*

"To be a man of flesh and blood, that is, one of those we call fictitious, which is the same thing . . .": here we have one of the most patent of all Unamunian paradoxes. It was formulated by him as an answer to the question: What is the "intimate" (the "true," the "eternal," the "creative," the "poetic") reality of an individual? We may be tempted to dismiss the paradox with the excuse that it was only meant to provoke the rationalists' wrath. But if we followed our rational drive, our understanding of Unamuno's world view would be seriously impaired. The equating of fiction—or, more exactly, a certain type of fiction—with reality, plays a fundamental role in Unamuno's thought. After all, the paradox in question is closely related to the Unamunian doctrine of the dream and of the relation between God and creation—or the author and his characters. It was observed (chapter two) that this relation was similar to the one that existed between the dreamer and the dreamed. But since this idea of a "fictitious entity" is more clearly presented in his theory and practice of the novel than anywhere else, we shall turn now to an analysis of the meaning of the Unamunian novel—of the novels Unamuno wrote and of the comments he made on them.

Novels are written for various reasons: because one is a born novelist—just as one is a born poet or mathematician; because one wishes to make a name for one's self as a writer at a time when the novel has become the most widely read of all the literary genres; in order to eke out a living; in order to articulate one or more theses on the nature of man or on the condition of society; because man (or certain men) enjoy inventing characters and relating adventures; or for a combination of all these reasons. But why did Unamuno write novels? We must exclude the first reason, for Unamuno was not "a born novelist" in the way that Flaubert, Pérez Galdós, Dickens, or Dostoevski were, or in the way that Mauriac, Faulkner, Cela, or Graham Greene are. The second reason cannot be entirely dismissed, since it is operative in Unamuno—at least in the sense of contributing to the expansion of his personality. Yet it cannot be the determining factor, since a similar "expansion" of his own personality was achieved more successfully in his journalism than in his novel writing. The third reason has some importance if we rely on certain declarations of the author himself—for example, those found in some of his letters. But it does not explain why he adopted his rather peculiar novelistic technique. The fourth reason presents a delicate problem, since it is feasible to extract several "theses" from Unamuno's novels. It is not difficult, however, to see that Unamuno's novels are not *romans á thèse* in the strict sense in which some of Zola's purported to be; or as those of Feodor Gladkov or Silone have been. The fifth reason is more basic than it at first appears, because the production of novels would be impossible without some sort of creative drive and the psychological satisfaction that it provides for the novelist. This last reason, however, is too general to clarify the most specific traits in Unamuno's novelistic production, so that it must be taken only with reservation.

Are we then to conclude that, at bottom, Unamuno wrote his novels for no reason, or that only a combination of all the afore-mentioned reasons will adequately answer our question? That would be either too easy or too trivial. Therefore, let us look for specifically "Unamunian" reasons that will not exclude any of the others, but may prove to be more substantial than all of them combined.

Two of these "deeper" reasons present themselves to any careful reader of Unamuno's novels. On the one hand, as Julián Marías has pointed out, Unamuno seems to wish to make of the novel a means of access to human reality. This is tantamount to making of the novel a kind of epistemological tool for the under-standing of this reality. On the other hand, Unamuno seemed to presuppose that reality cannot be defined as "what it is," nor fiction defined as "what it is not." To him fiction and reality were two aspects of a single entity that could only be understood from the "creational" point of view—from the "dream as creation" point of view.

Both reasons are important, but we feel that the latter is more basic or, at least, more "Unamunian" than the former. Let us examine them both.

Marías' thesis has obviously been influenced by what I may call "Ortega y Gasset's epistemology of human reality." According to it, human life is not definable, nor even describable, as a "thing," or a "substance" of any sort. It is best described as a kind of novel (or perhaps drama). One of its fundamental in-gredients is, as some existentialists would put it, "self-projection," the fact that man always "anticipates" what he is going to become. It follows that fictional lives, far from being nonentities, are enti-ties of a rather peculiar kind since description of what they "are" is likely to cast some light on human beings that really exist. Thus we can say that the novel—the "personal" or "existential" novel, as Unamuno foreshadowed and anticipated it—possesses a methodological value. Although the description of fictitious entities cannot be conceptualized without the help of a previous "metaphysics of human reality," it nevertheless proves to be extremely useful as a first step toward the development of an "existential analytic" of human existence.

The above thesis seems to fit a number of characteristic traits in Unamuno's novels, as well as a number of Unamuno's own confessions of his aims as a novelist. There is no doubt that the characters in Unamuno's novels are not simply "human natures," always ready to respond in the same basic ways to natural, social, or human environment. The physical appearance, the dress, the actual gestures, the physical background or even the plot are not the important elements of novels. They ought not to be the important part, Unamuno contended, in any novel worth the name. What mattered in a novel was exactly the same thing that mattered in "reality": the fact, namely, that it dealt with "real beings"—or, as Unamuno often wrote, with "tragic agonizers" (meaning, of course, "fighters"). These characters are, or should be, true subjects who reveal themselves to us at certain critical moments, and who do so, just as we and our "actual" fellow humans do, "by a cry, by a sudden action, by a revealing phrase." Only in this way are we given their "intimate reality," which can no longer be ontologically distinguished from that of a "real being" since it has been agreed that the so-called "real beings" as well as those we suppose fictional, possess the same type of "reality."

There are many passages in Unamuno's novels that support this view of the world of human "fiction." Furthermore, he was himself very generous with explanations of this point. He claimed that a true novelist ought to avoid all false "realism." He emphasized that the characters he depicted—or more exactly, in whose innards he poked about—were truly intimate because of what they revealed of themselves. With the "soul of their soul" laid bare, Unamuno held, they were indistinguishable from truly existing beings. If we feel, however, that Unamuno's *modus explanandi* is obscure, or unnecessarily paradoxical, we may turn to his *modus operandi*. It will make his ideas on the subject, if not acceptable, at least clear.

Let us consider briefly four of his novels: *Mist* (*Niebla;* 1914), *Abel Sánchez* (1917), *Three Exemplary Novels and a Prologue* (*Tres novelas ejemplares y un prólogo;* 1920), and *Aunt Tula* (*La tía Tula;* 1921). All "circumstances" in them are reduced to a minimum—if not simply eliminated. Sensations and emotions, predominant in "classical" novels, become "reactions," strictly personal in tone. Unamuno does not write, for example, "Augusto breathed a sigh of relief," but "Augusto felt calm— entranced." Even when apparently most trivial, Unamuno's dialogue does not create "atmosphere" or "background." It is not a way of describing the "environment." It is a way of shouting, cursing, repenting, and complaining—of laying one's self bare. As a consequence, the characters are not of the flesh but they do have, as Unamuno pointed out, skeletons—"personal skeletons," of course. In this manner, all exteriority—circumstances, environment, even the plot itself—is done away with; the "intimate realities," which shine through the merely schematic descriptions, are creative to the extent that they are progressively compounded in the narrative process. "Reality" and "fiction" are inextricably mixed and the question of what allows us to distinguish between them becomes meaningless. The "depths of the soul," the "throbbing innards," the "chill in the bones," the "naked passions" are terms used by Unamuno not only to describe what his characters feel, but also, and above all, to erase the traces of any dividing line between the "material" and the "spiritual," between "flesh" and "soul."

The reader acquainted with Unamuno's novels will have noticed that I have not mentioned either his first or his last: *Peace in War* (*Paz en la guerra;* 1897) or *Saint Emmanuel the Good, Martyr* (*San Manuel Bueno, mártir;* 1933). Is this because they do not follow the same procedure, or—with the author's pardon—the same "pattern"? To a certain extent, yes. Unamuno has said of the first that it belonged to the "oviparous" species—the species of novels cultivated by writers who "make a plan in order to hatch a nucleus." Of the other novels, except the last one, he has said that they belong to the "viviparous" species—the species cultivated by writers who abstain from all carefully drawn plans and allow the novel to make its own plan as it is written. Now, although Unamuno's last novel represents to a considerable degree the culmination of his work along the lines of the "personal novel" and of the "viviparous" method, it also represents the beginning of a new way of writing novels. This way is neither straightforwardly "viviparous" nor elaborately "oviparous," neither exclusively "personal" nor purely "environmental." I suspect that the changes that Unamuno's *Saint Emmanuel the Good, Martyr* reveals are not confined to his method of writing novels, but apply also to the new direction of his philosophical enquiries. In *Peace in War,* Unamuno had proclaimed that we live—or must live—at peace within war. In the "intermediate" novels we are often told that there is a perpetual struggle between peace and war, a struggle that explains the sustained tension between characters, and of each of them with himself. It would seem that in *Saint Emmanuel* men are invited to live at war within peace. A most interesting change in thought, or at least in mood. Therefore, if the idea of the tragic sense of life, so characteristic of Unamuno's thought, has not entirely disappeared in that novel, it would seem to have changed direction. From what the tormented yet calm protagonist of *Saint Emmanuel* does and thinks, we may conclude that although to live is still to struggle, one no longer struggles only to remain in the struggle, but in order to plunge into that "lake of the eternal" where Valverde de Lucena—the "submerged town"—lives so peacefully. A year after *Saint Emmanuel* was published, Unamuno made a resounding speech, on the occasion of his installation as "Perpetual Rector" of the University of Salamanca. The contents of this speech resemble, curiously enough, the contents of the short story; they both emphasize peace and restfulness. If Unamuno had been able to develop in the direction indicated, it is quite possible that his philosophical thought would have undergone drastic modifications, and that the present book, and not only the present chapter, would have been quite differently written.

For other reasons, *Peace in War* and *Saint Emmanuel the Good, Martyr* are exceptions to Unamuno's most characteristic approach to the problems of fiction. I have, accordingly, excluded them from our previous analysis. It would be unfair, however, to ignore them entirely. After all, the latter novel represents as much a beginning of what might have developed as a culmination of what was actually performed. As for the former, there are certain readily noticeable modes of expression beneath the obviously "oviparous" structure which belie Unamuno's own description of its nature. There is, for example, in the novel a persistent avoidance of all more or less "realistic" description of characters, even if the "bottom of the [characters'] souls" is not yet quite evident.

This last point deserves further elucidation. If we read *Peace in War* without much care, we find it very similar to many of the so-called (rather loosely so) "realistic nineteenth-century novels." It is quite obviously full of circumstantial description, historical references, many of them exact (as in the arrival of the king and his reception by the peasants). We find details of the past of some characters (for example, of José María de Arana's life). We also find vivid descriptions of events (witness the very "realistic" battle scenes). As if all this were not enough, many of the characters cross paths again and again, thus creating an "atmosphere." But on reflection we discover that the means of conveying all this differs from the "traditional" way in several crucial respects. Two examples will, I hope, suffice.

The first has been pointed out by Marías in his analysis of the novel. It refers to the account of the club members' arrival in the back room of Pedro Antonio's store. Each character has his own characteristic gesture—puffing, rubbing hands together, cleaning spectacles, taking off his coat. Yet these gestures are neither circumstantial nor merely "habitual," but truly "intimate" ones. If the objection is raised that the characters are still conditioned by the strictly personal background—which includes typical psychological traits no less than physical surroundings—the second example may be more convincing. It is a passage—by no means the only one of this type in the novel—in which the very existence of "things" is questioned by the author's peculiar way of describing them. Here Unamuno gives an account of the fear felt by Ignacio "when he hears the first shot." How does Unamuno convey this fear? Simply by writing that "the landscape began to melt before his eyes." This way of writing may today be trite, but in the midst of a still overpowering "realism" it was a novelty. For the landscape is not presented as a thing that surrounds the character, but as something that manifests itself in a rather astonishing manner: by "melting." Other passages in the same novel confirm our point: the landscape that surrounds Pachico is not one way or another, not clearly and unequivocally described by the novelist. It is not composed of one kind of tree or another or traversed by this or that river; it is something that flows from itself, blending with the individual whom it ought, in principle, to serve as mere "circumstance." To sum up: instead of beginning with the "exterior" in order to provide a frame for a character, the exterior is personified, tuned to the rhythm of the character's own existence.

This is, of course, entirely different from those methods that "realistic" authors like Pérez Galdós sometimes employ—for example, at the beginning of his novel *The Spendthrift* (*La de Bringas*). I have written "sometimes," because Pérez Galdós' realism is, to begin with, highly problematical, being often more "Unamunian" than he himself suspected. Furthermore, Unamuno's originality in this respect does not preclude his participation in the tradition of the Spanish novel which runs from *Don Quijote* down through not a few of Pérez Galdós' works (*Mercy* [*Misericordia*] being a revealing example). A substantial element of this tradition is Unamunian *avant la lettre*. For most Spanish authors the novel is not a mirror carried along a highway, not the reflection of an impressionistic universe, and not even the single recounting of a series of human emotions. For them the novel is rather the description of a universe that is, at bottom, personal in nature. Unamuno continued, then, a certain literary tradition, but did not limit himself to repeating it. He gave it new life, and since he was a philosopher as much as, if not more than, a novelist, he managed finally to make it aware of itself.

29   *The world as a divine novel*

As early as *Peace in War,* therefore, Unamuno's characters are described not as individuals (in the modern sense of the word 'individual') nor as psychological types, but as "little Gods." And this brings us to our second "basic reason" for Unamuno's novel writing—and to the central theme of the present chapter: his wish to prove in a nondiscursive way that all dividing lines between "fiction" and "reality" must be erased once and for all.

This theme is, as we have pointed out, closely related to the one discussed in an earlier chapter: the essential type of "relation" that exists between an author and the characters he describes—or rather, creates. This relationship, analogous to the one that, according to Unamuno, existed between God and man, can be detailed in terms of the already mentioned dependency of "dreamer" and "the dreamed." This dependency is not a simple one. As a matter of fact, the term 'dependency' is rather inadequate in this connection. Just as the characters in a writer's novels rebel against his efforts to make them puppets of his own fancy, or mere loudspeakers of his opinions, the writer, in his turn, rebels against the possibility that his Author—or "the Dreamer"—may direct him according to His fancy. True enough, a writer may feel at times that he is living at the mercy of God's dream, a dream on the point of becoming a nightmare. Unamuno alluded to this feeling —he was obviously quite troubled by it—on several occasions. The appearance and disappearance of characters (and, for that matter, of all events) often seemed to him to mirror the movements of a "divine chess set," so much so that characters, events, and author seemed like nothing so much as pieces and pawns in a grandiose game. But this impression of Unamuno's vanished at once, for however closely the lives of the characters seem linked to the author's dreams, there was always the possibility that, as Unamuno noted in *Love and Pedagogy,* they could ad-lib. Like actors on a stage, men could often take advantage of the author's negligence to slip in some of their own words among those indicated in the script—this, of course, as a stopgap measure until they had a chance to write their own plays. And if they were caught ad-libbing, there would at least be the possibility of modifying the "text" by the inflection of their own "voices"—by their own "accent."

So if man's reality is, in a way, the contents of somebody else's dream, it is not entirely subject to the Dreamer's whims. What we call "a dream" is, in fact, a struggle between the Dreamer and the dreamed. This accounts for the fact that "to be real" means to be dreamed and at the same time to strive to escape the Dreamer's grasp. The dependency between the Dreamer and the dreamed is, basically, an interdependency, for even when the person dreamed finds the dream in which he lives most oppressive, he is still aware that he is capable of influencing the life, and hence the dreams, of his Dreamer—or his Author, for to dream and to create are two sides of the same coin.

Since the characters created by the novelist are related to the novelist just as the latter is related to God, we may be tempted to conclude that a "dream hierarchy" exists which could replace the "hierarchy of being," one in which man would occupy the middle point between two extremes: God, and the characters in novels. This conclusion, however, would be a rash generalization. On the one hand, there are times when characters and author seem to play on the same field, both dependent upon God's dreams (God could be described here as the personification of "intrareality" and of "intrahistory" in the Unamunian sense). We might then conceive of God as the Supreme Poet or the Supreme Novelist—

and that would be neither more nor less reasonable than imagining Him as the Supreme Watchmaker, the Supreme Geometrician, or the Supreme Calculator. "To dream the world" would be a way (perhaps not more metaphorical than most others) of saying "to make the world," or "to create the world." Human beings and the fictitious entities created by novelists would have the same type of being; they would both be describable only in terms of _who_ they are (and not of _what_ they are). And since God was also, for Unamuno, "each man's dream," there would be no way of telling who dreams whom precisely because everyone would be dreaming everyone else. On the other hand, all these realities are mixed together, and hence resist organization into any hierarchy on account of a presupposition that Unamuno believed to be plain fact: the impossibility of distinguishing between contemplation and action, between telling (or narrating) and doing—and, in general, as we have seen in other instances, between any opposing terms. Thus it would be incorrect to distinguish between an author and the characters he creates. The entire book—Unamuno would prefer to say "the entire cry"—entitled _How a Novel Is Made_ (_Cómo se hace una novela_) repeats this point again and again. In this book we see how the character of a novel lives obsessed by the character in another novel. Their deaths should coincide, and for this reason whenever the former reads about what is happening to the latter he lives in a constant state of agony. The lives of the two characters are inextricably intertwined. Should we say that they are both real or that they are both fictitious? Physically speaking, of course, they are fictitious. But as persons, one is as real as is the other. And both are as real, or as fictitious, as their common dreamer, the novelist who created them and was constantly shaped, and therefore created, by them in the process. No true novel can be dismissed as "mere literature." In point of fact, there is no such thing as "mere literature." When a novel can be included in such a category, it is because it is not a novel or, for that matter, an author's book, but a mere collection of meaningless words. To be sure, Unamuno could not prove, and did not attempt to prove, that "true literature is life and true life literature." But such an apothegm becomes clearer when we try to understand that unless a character is a puppet—and hence no character at all—he is, in a way, as real as his author. The so-called real persons cannot be distinguished, except by their lack of personality, from the so-called fictitious ones. Both live at the heart of that "mist" to which Unamuno insistently refers—and which may be understood as a further manifestation of that common realm in which all things live, at war and ever seeking peace. As a consequence, the Unamunian theory and practice of the novel appears as a fundamental aspect of his philosophy of tragedy—that tragedy made up of the dialectic of hope and despair.

It would be easy to argue that Unamuno's insistence on the lack of distinction between fiction and reality was merely the expression of a desire to confuse things, or at best to invert all relationships—between God and Nature, Nature and man, man and God, man and his creations, and so on. From a strictly conceptual point of view such an argument would be perfect. It would, however, miss the point, for Unamuno does not here pretend to explain reality, but to make it "coherent." To bring it closer to our experience as authors and readers of novels. From this point of view we can say that the characters in novels are the author's "dreams," while admitting that these characters "should speak for themselves," and be "spontaneous." These two assertions are not too difficult to reconcile provided we admit that the relative autonomy of these characters does not prevent their being ruled by the laws of a common world: the world of "reality-fiction." If the characters were simply fictitious, their independence of the author would be illusory; the author would always lead them by the hand. If they were merely real, on the other hand, their dependence on the author would be abolished; they would become so completely detached from him that they would no longer be characters, but "things."

This hybrid concept of "reality-fiction" offers a further advantage in that it allows us a new glimpse of the most persistent of all Unamunian themes: "the man of flesh and blood." It should by now be clear that this expression does not denote merely a biological entity *nor* a spiritual entity. These entities can be conceptualized by means of such categories as "the real," "the imaginary," and others of a similar kind. Men of flesh and blood, as people, cannot be so conceptualized. They do not belong to a definite order of being; they do not reveal themselves by being this or that, but by making, talking, suffering, enjoying and, of course, "agonizing." Now, these are the properties that belong both to "real people" and to characters in a story. If we still insist on using the verb 'to be' when speaking of them, it would be better to use it as a part of the expression 'the-will-to-be'. In the final analysis, it is the will-to-*be* as fully as possible—to be a person— that makes this "reality-fiction" the most authentic expression of the only truly human—and perhaps, divine—resource: ceaseless creativity, which is possibly another name for the Unamunian concept of "intrareality."

I have just written "human—and perhaps, divine." By forcing meanings—and interpretations—I might have written "human-divine." Has not Unamuno asked himself if the "intimate and supreme I" that he longed to be might not be God Himself? Has he not made it clear that whoever says "novelistic creation" is saying "theological and philosophical creation"? Has he not spoken of the consciousness of "my" body as if it were a "wave in the sea"? The reality of the world as God's dream is, apparently, a novel. But this novel is anchored in the ceaseless novelizing of mankind. A pawn in a divine game, mankind is ultimately, according to Unamuno, the substance of God's dream.

SEVEN

The Idea of Reality

30   The meanings of 'is real'

SOME PHILOSOPHERS have given the predicate 'is real' an explicit meaning; indeed, a substantial portion of their work is devoted to a clarification of the meaning of such a predicate. It was relatively easy for these philosophers to arrive at their conception or idea of reality. Thus, we can describe, or at least discuss, what 'is real' meant to Plato, Aristotle, Hume, or Kant. Other philosophers, however, have never given the question "What does 'is real' mean?" (or, in a more ontological vocabulary: "What is Reality?") an explicit answer. And yet they have nevertheless underwritten a conception or idea of reality; it is just that they have never expressed this idea in terms of analysis or definition. It was very difficult (although not impossible) for such philosophers to know what they felt, philosophically speaking, Reality was.

Unamuno belongs to this latter group. He was, in fact, one of its most typical members, for he never attempted to enlighten his readers as to the meaning (or meanings) he gave the predicate 'is real'. This is, by the way, one of the reasons why he has often been denied the status of philosopher. But this and all other reasons like it, in the main, are quite inconclusive, unless we have a very definite and rather narrow idea of what 'to be a philosopher' means. We may, of course, subscribe to a limited idea, but then neither Kierkegaard nor Nietzsche could be treated as philosophers. If, as I believe, Kierkegaard and Nietzsche were philosophers, then Unamuno was also one. This is why we may submit his apparently nonphilosophical ideas and arguments to a philosophical clarification.

Unamuno fought unceasingly against all abstractions, even while proclaiming the need of paying heed to "realities." As I have said, however, he never made clear what he meant by 'reality'. Philosophers may claim that he even did just the opposite: confused the issue by pointing out that that supreme reality of his—"the man of flesh and blood"—was also a kind of fiction created by a dreamer, at the same time announcing that he considered the fictitious characters in novels to be also, in a very important sense, "real." It would seem, then, that the meaning of the predicate 'is real' in Unamuno's thought was either hopelessly ambiguous or unnecessarily unfathomable. There is apparently no rational approach to the problem, so that the only thing to do is to repeat or reformulate some of Unamuno's contradictions and paradoxes.

On a closer inspection of his writings we find that although Unamuno never attempted to define the meaning of the predicate 'is real', he was always intent upon representing (by means of descriptions and intuitions) the form and substance of "true realities." Furthermore, he refused to admit that any of the metaphysical entities hailed by some philosophers—matter, mind, ideas, values, and so forth—were in any fundamental sense "real." With the help of these descriptions and intuitions we can reconstruct to some degree Unamuno's idea of reality.

31   What reality is not

I will begin by recapitulating Unamuno's reactions to some of the traditional metaphysical entities that philosophers have misused by always presenting them in the guise of absolutes.

Since Unamuno insisted so earnestly on the idea that all beings have "souls" and "innards"—although these are "corporeal souls and innards"—we may suppose that he thought appearances concealed the "true realities," and that the latter were like absolute beings hidden in the core of phenomena. But this supposition would prove to be incorrect. Unamuno never defended a substantialist philosophy as against a phenomenalistic one, nor did he ever pit the latter against the former. For Unamuno there is no thing-in-itself, no metaphysically absolute nature beyond or beneath sensible things. There is nothing that corresponds to Ideas, Substances, or Forms. Things-in-themselves are for him far too abstract and too remote when compared with the "concrete realities" with which we come in contact and to which we cling—such realities as "men of flesh and blood," *"this* character in a novel," *"this* landscape," *"this* star in the sky." To a certain extent, if any 'ism' fits Unamuno at all, it is "radical empiricism." For, whenever Unamuno seems about to accept some metaphysical entity—e.g., the Schopenhauerian Will—it is only in order to strike an immediate blow against all that is abstract in it. Philosophers have often sought "what is most real," but they have always ended by depriving it of reality *simpliciter*. It is most probable that Unamuno would have subscribed to Goethe's well-known verses:

> Natur hat weder Kern noch Schale
> Alles ist sie mit einemale

("Nature has neither shell nor kernel, it is everything at once"), provided the German poet was ready to include in Nature things he had originally not meant to include.

Nor is reason—or, if one prefers, Reason—real. The world is not crystal-clear, not logical. It is not transparent, but resistant and opaque. When Hegel said that the rational was real and the real rational, he was not speaking, Unamuno surmised, as a philosopher, and much less as a "man of flesh and blood"; he spoke as a bureaucrat. To be sure, reason must not be discarded; Unamuno said more than once that "the reprisals of reason" were absolutely necessary because they bring us into abrupt contact with doubt, and without doubt we cannot stumble upon reality. But reason-in-itself is far from being a real entity: it is one of the extremes between which "we move and are." Nor can the irrational-in-itself be real, for analogous reasons, because to say that the world is, at bottom, irrational, or is *"the* Irrational," is to seek comfort and shun tragedy, that is to say, life. "The Rational" and "the Irrational" are, therefore, nothing more than the metaphorical hypostases invented by philosophers in order to exorcise their spleen—or in order to assuage their desperation.

32   What reality is like

To the above negations others might be added, but those already noted will suffice for our purpose. We can now turn to more positive statements about the basic characteristics of reality. Needless to say, we shall not find "propositions" about the nature of reality in Unamuno's works. On the other hand, we can find numerous descriptions of "what is truly real." These descriptions are patent because of Unamuno's preference for certain terms that he systematically used whenever he meant to convey the impression that he was face to face with true realities. A "linguistic approach" to our problem—in a rather broad sense of the term 'linguistic'—is inescapable; I will therefore attempt to reconstruct Unamuno's idea of reality on the basis of an examination of his language.

Above all, the innermost is real for Unamuno. Words such as 'innards', 'intimate', 'pithy', 'bones', 'marrow', 'mesentery', 'hidden', 'chasm', 'abyss', 'bottom', 'depth', 'unfathomable', 'substantial', 'soul', and the like play a fundamental role in Unamuno's thought. These are not, however, terms that purport to designate constitutionally "hidden" realities, and even less "things-in-themselves," since they always refer to what has a decidedly visible, tangible, and palpable aspect. The identification of the real with something "metaphysical," or with something "within," "beneath," or "beyond" appearances is one thing; the constant "going inward" of the real so often emphasized by Unamuno is another. The innermost is not hidden, nor is it merely on the surface. Strictly speaking, it cannot be said to fall into any of the categories currently used by many philosophers—being as opposed to appearance, reality to its manifestations, noumena to phenomena, and so forth since it possesses a peculiar *status:* that of manifesting itself *according* to the degree of its intimacy. Not by constituting the foundation of the apparent, nor by being what is apparent, but by becoming apparent *as* foundation. Or, to put it another way: the innermost is the "within" of things to the degree that it is deprived of a "without." For this reason it has two constant characteristics. On the one hand, it is something that moves with a movement similar to that of living—its throbbing, trembling, and pulsating can be perceived. This is why the innards of which Unamuno spoke are always "palpitating innards." On the other hand, it is something that never slackens, that flows ceaselessly: the innermost is inexhaustible. This is why it can be thought of as the analogue of certain physical processes—jet, source, spring, fountain—which frequently, and not by chance, provide the subject matter of poetic description. Like the *physis* of the pre-Socratics, the innermost flows perennially from its own reservoir. Thus we may conclude that the real is always the intrareal—just as history was, as we have seen, intrahistory—if we always keep in mind that there is no strict opposition between an "intra" and an "extra," nor even less, a reduction of one to the other. For once the battle has subsided for lack of combatants. If the innermost struggles, as does everything, with itself, it does not do so in the sense that its being opposes its becoming, or vice versa: the opposition takes the same form as that in which our intimacy—all open and palpitating—fights with itself. Thus what we call "the true reality" is not matter or spirit, flesh or soul, because it can be, and usually is, both. Intramatter is just as real as intraspirit. Only "matter as such" and "spirit as such" are not real; they are mere abstractions lacking in movement, in flowing and overflowing force, devoid of incessantly palpitating intimacy.

The "serious" is real and with it, above all, the dense (*lo denso*). It is easy to see to what extent everything that is swift, lucid, voluble, playful, insinuating, suggestive, allusive, and ironical is alien to the cosmos of Unamuno. But this does not mean that his is a dull universe drowned in circumspection and composure; on the contrary, it continually erupts with shouts, imprecations, and even altercations. Nonetheless, all this is somehow contained within the tightly packed, firm silence of which we said the needlework pattern of Unamuno's life consisted. This seriousness manifests itself in two basic ways. On the one hand, as something possessing a tightly woven, tough texture, hard, if not impossible, to break. The real, to the degree that it is serious, is something vigorous; hard—frequently coarse and unpleasant—and consequently just the opposite of anything that is smooth, fine, polished, pretty, flexible, graceful. On the other hand, the real shows itself as something possessing corporeality or, as Unamuno so often said, bulk; the tangible is real and, above all, the palpable is real. The models for these characterizations of the real are evidently certain physical objects—I would almost say, macrophysical ones. But they are also certain sensations whose grossness is not always to be confused with roughness. Although predominantly "physical," the traits of the real that we have mentioned are not the exclusive attributes of matter; ideals too, if they truly are ideals instead of dissolving abstractions, possess, according to Unamuno, this seriousness and density that make them firm and bulky, almost corporeal. Like the innermost, the serious and bulky are to be found at the bottom of all that is material *and* all that is spiritual inasmuch as they have a consistency, that is, a density.

The abrupt is real, if it is understood not as one of the many possible synonyms for what is harsh and uneven, but as denoting a mode of being characterized by discontinuity. Here the abrupt is, then, a "leap." To a certain extent it may be understood by analogy with the Kierkegaardian notion "the leap." Like that notion, the Unamunian intuition of a leap is equally opposed to any principle of continuity or to a mediation that would reconcile opposites. In philosophical terms, it is equally opposed to Leibnizianism and Hegelianism. The real does not stretch out in a continuous line. Nor does it constitute a logico-metaphysical system that is dependent upon a foreseeable Becoming explained by means of some "dialectical method." What I have suggested here as "explanation" is rather a "decision"—and one that presupposes absurdity and paradox. And yet, the "real" man—the "authentic" man—is not the one who hides behind his social cover, his everyday gestures and conventional words, but he who reveals himself abruptly in all his contradictory being. And reality itself, for Unamuno, is not a more or less rough stratum beneath a smooth surface, but at one and the same time the polished *and* the rough. It will be seen that here again there is for Unamuno no kernel beneath the shell, but a kernel and a shell viewed in cross section from the moment of their birth to the moment of their death.

What Unamuno sometimes called "the contradictory," and what is more properly labeled "the constant conflict of opposites," is also real. The real exists in a state of combat—at war with an opposite and at war with itself. Here we have one of the pillars—not to say the axis—of this book. Let us only recall that for Unamuno war was so fundamental that, not content with declaring it ever-present, he concluded that it makes war on itself and, furthermore, that it fights continually with its antagonist, peace, giving no quarter. Peace is to be found in the heart of war and vice versa: without war there is no possible peace. The struggle between opposites and of each opposite with itself is not, therefore, the result of a logical contradiction; it is the very core of the tragic dynamism of life. The motor of this interminable movement is a conflict whose ontological nature must always be kept in mind: it derives from the eagerness of each being to remain itself while striving to become what other beings are, and hence, longing to cease being what it is. The formal pattern of this struggle is the opposition between the limited and the unlimited. This opposition is apparent everywhere, but it is most obvious in the struggles that Unamuno has most often described: those between fictitious characters and their creators, between what one intends to be and what one is, between man and God.

That which lasts—or, if one prefers, that which is everlasting —is also real. Not, of course, the intemporal and abstractly eternal, but the permanently concrete. This last can be understood in two ways. First, as something whose permanence is being continuously produced or created; true permanence is, Unamuno believes, the result of an effort, of an act of will, of a *conatus,* to such an extent that there is no fundamental difference between being and wishing to be. Second, as something whose duration is constantly threatened by annihilation; just as war is the guarantee of peace, death—the imminence of death—is the guarantee of life. To last forever is not to go on existing, to continue to be; it is the unceasing conquest of its own being. This explains why for Unamuno to live was primarily "to agonize," that is, to fight against death.

And finally, whatever feels or, as Unamuno has written, "whatever suffers, has pity and yearns," is real. This has led him to identify reality with consciousness and even to maintain that "the only substantial reality is consciousness." By this time it should no longer be necessary to warn the reader against the tendency to interpret such a phrase in any idealistic sense. Unamuno is not an idealist or a realist for the simple reason that for him suffering, pitying, and relishing constitute ways of being real that affect both the consciousness *and* things. The mode of being of things cannot be deduced, even by analogy, from that of the consciousness: "to feel" is, strictly speaking, "to react"—and to react strongly, with vigor and vehemence. The universe *qua* "sensitive being" is, therefore, a universe *qua* active being which changes, transforms itself, struggles to be, and even "despairs" of ever being what it wishes to be. Just as the attributes of bulk and palpableness may be imputed to ideas, so that of consciousness may be applied to things, if, of course, we avoid the error of supposing that we are only projecting our consciousness upon them. Therefore, true reality is never passivity. What has been called "consciousness" is, in ultimate terms, a means—however insufficient and equivocal—of recognizing that only what refuses to cease to be really is.

Notes

A preliminary note

IN MY PRESENTATION OF Unamuno's thought, I have taken into account all his writing available in book form and some still uncollected. Most can be found in the books listed in the first section of the bibliography.

There are two reasons why I have not indicated the places in Unamuno's writings to which the reader might turn for the material quoted or referred to in the text. First, because I have tried to "absorb" Unamuno's ideas and present them only after they were sufficiently "digested." Second, and most important, because any reference to Unamunian texts would be incomplete unless it were tiresomely detailed. Unamuno presented his central ideas frequently and in the most varied places. He drew attention to this tendency of his to repeat his themes and ideas in an article that appeared in the review *Caras y Caretas* of Buenos Aires on September 23, 1923. There he remarked that "the greatest writers have spent their lives reiterating a few points, always the same ones; polishing and re-polishing them, seeking the most perfect, the definitive expression of them." It is hardly necessary to add that this idea about reiteration was, in its turn, reiterated by Unamuno on several occasions.

Although I have taken into account almost all of Unamuno's vast production, at the beginning of each of the notes for the seven chapters I have indicated various of his works in which the material discussed in that chapter appears in particular concentration. In the remaining part of these chapter notes I have done no more than point out certain secondary sources that treat in full detail the various points debated in the text of the chapter.

I have also clarified briefly some terms or problems with which the English reader may not be familiar. But I have not offered additional information about Spanish authors mentioned in the text—for example, the members of the Generation of 1898 and the generation immediately preceding it—because what I might have added there would not have been directly important to an understanding of this book. The reader may easily avail himself of sources (encyclopedias and histories of literature) which will supply the required information. The same applies to other than Spanish authors mentioned occasionally. In most instances these names—Schopenhauer or Kierkegaard—are well enough known. For the rest no more need be known of an author for the purposes of this book than what is adduced in the text.

The translations of passages from Unamuno's works have been done directly from the original.

Note to chapter one

In the third section of the bibliography I have included only those works that are of interest for the understanding and interpretation of Unamuno's philosophical thought, or his literary style whenever this is intimately linked with the expression of that thought. Some of these works contain biographical data. For more detailed information about Unamuno's life the reader is referred to Luis S. Granjel's *Retrato de Unamuno* (Madrid, 1957) and to A. Sánchez-Barbudo's *Estudios sobre Unamuno y Machado* (Madrid, 1959), pages 13–198.

From among the multitude of studies on the Spanish Generation of 1898 I particularly recommend Pedro Laín Entralgo's *La generación del noventa y ocho* (Madrid, 1945) and the anthology, *The Generation of 1898 and After* (New York-Toronto, 1960), prepared by Beatrice P. Patt and Martin Nozick. This latter work contains brief introductory notes in English which head the various Spanish texts by Angel Ganivet, Ramón María del Valle-Inclán, Pío Baroja, *Azorín,* Antonio Machado, and others.

The term *Krausistas* designates a group of philosophers, notably Julián Sanz del Río (1814–1869) and Francisco Giner de los Ríos (1839–1915), who were influenced by the German idealist Karl Christian Friederich Krause (1781–1832) and various of his disciples. Spanish Krausism, however, was much more than a simple adaptation of a foreign philosophical system, with a complexity and an autonomous growth of its own. The reader may consult Pierre Jobit's *Les éducateurs de l'Espagne moderne,* 2 vols. (*I. Les krausistes; II. Lettres inédites de J. Sanz del Río*) (Paris, 1936) and Juan López-Morillas' *El krausismo español* (Mexico, 1956).

Francisco Ayala's idea about Unamuno may be found in the article "La perspectiva hispánica," included in his book *Razón del mundo* (Buenos Aires, 1944), pages 117–164.

Unamuno's "religious crisis," placed in or about the year 1897, has been studied in detail by A. Sánchez-Barbudo, *op. cit.;* see especially pages 43–79.

"Silence" in the life of Unamuno, and his aspiration to "plunge into the eternal" (*zambullirse en lo eterno*) which he expressed in his work on numerous occasions, are a proof that together with the conflictive mode of our author there is also a contemplative one. I have alluded to this latter mode in the present book, particularly in chapter six. The contemplative mode in Unamuno's life and work has been carefully studied by Carlos Blanco Aguinaga in *El Unamuno contemplativo* (Mexico, 1959).

Note to chapter two

The basic works for this chapter are *Del sentimento trágico de la vida, Ensayos V, Mi religión y otros ensayos, Rosario de sonetos líricos, Rimas de dentro,* and *Niebla.* The first of these is the most important, but, as I have mentioned above, Unamuno constantly returned to the same ideas from various angles, so that there are few of his writings that do not contain some reference to one of his most central themes: the reality of the man of flesh and blood, and the relation of this man to the world and to God. Then, too, the theme of the perpetual tension between opposites is not just an idea with Unamuno, but also a form of expression. This is why all of Unamuno's work is pertinent in this respect.

With regard to the much-debated question of the relation between Unamuno and Kierkegaard, it should be noted that very likely the first discovered the writings of the second only after he had developed ideas of his own similar to those of Kierkegaard. At the same time it is also likely that the reading of Kierkegaard helped Unamuno reaffirm and develop these ideas. The problem has been dealt with by P. Mesnard and R. Ricard, and above all by F. Meyer, in those works by these authors mentioned in the third section of the bibliography.

A thorough examination of the influences exercised upon Unamuno throughout a lifetime of reading would demand a separate book. He was a voracious reader who easily assimilated all that he read, and retained most of it for a long time, thanks to a prodigious memory. Furthermore, his reading was tremendously varied. Unamuno read whatever came his way, and this was no small amount; he read classical and modern authors, poets and philosophers, historians and scientists. And he read not only books, but countless articles and essays in reviews and newspapers. Of the philosophers, Unamuno read the greater part of those most influential in his day and ken with a passionate interest— Kant, Hegel, Schopenhauer, Spencer, and also William James and others. He read materialists and spiritualists, realists and idealists. But once the influence of this reading has been established, the most important point to remember is that "absorption" best characterizes the method of Unamuno's reading. Even when he attacked them, he made those writers that he read "his" and, at times, even more securely "his" the harsher and more severe the attack. That Unamuno so often mentioned his reading in what he wrote, even the most recent of it—in many of his essays he would speak of books he was currently reading—should not lead us to the conclusion that there was a simple cause-and-effect relationship between these current readings and his own ideas of the moment. There was rather what might best be called a "resonance" between them—a concept as fertile as it is hard to define.

Note to chapter three

For the fullest understanding of this chapter, besides *Del sentimiento trágico de la vida* and *La agonía del cristianismo*—and the latter is a basic source for Unamuno's ideas on Christianity and history—all of those works must be kept in mind wherein the desire for an "eternity one is constantly striving for" is expressed, which appears in both of Unamuno's modes: that of perpetual tension or conflict and that of perpetual contemplation—and quite possibly in the dialogue between the two. In this respect, see *Paz en la guerra* and *San Manuel Bueno, mártir, Ensayos I, II, V* (and in this last volume of essays, particularly the one entitled "¡Plenitud de plenitudes y todo plenitud!"), *Mi religión y otros ensayos, Rosario de sonetos líricos,* and *Vida de Don Quijote y Sancho.* See also *El Cristo de Velázquez* and at least some of the poems in *Romancero del destierro.*

The manner in which Unamuno used—and, consciously or not, falsified—the Spinozian notion of *conatus* has been studied by François Meyer in his book *L'ontologie de Miguel de Unamuno* (Paris, 1955), pages 5 ff.

I have used the expression "The Great Chain of Being" as detailed in the well-known book by A. O. Lovejoy, *The Great Chain of Being* (1936), but in a more limited sense. The Hellenistic, the Christian, and the Hellenic-Christian "doctrinal complexes" have been considerably simplified in my exposition, but there was no need to treat them *in extenso* in order to set down Unamuno's attitude toward them.

The quotation from V. Nabokov is from his novel *Invitation to a Beheading.*

Note to chapter four

For this chapter, the basic texts are *Vida de Don Quijote y Sancho* and the appendix to *Del sentimiento trágico de la vida* entitled

"Don Quijote en la tragicomedia europea contemporánea." The reader is also referred to *Ensayos I, II* (in this last see particularly the essay "¡Adentro!"), *VII,* and the collection of essays *De esto y aquello,* Volume III. Certain differences between *Ensayos I* and *Vida de Don Quijote y Sancho* have been omitted because they were not pertinent to the exposition of our thesis. A great number of Unamuno's ideas on Spain appear in the descriptions of landscape in his "travel books." See, for instance, *Por tierras de Portugal y España, Andanzas y visiones españoles,* and the posthumous collection, *Paisajes del alma.* For Unamuno's interest in South American authors, see *De esto y aquello I.*

The bibliography on the so-called "problem of Spain" is without end. Closely connected with the discussions of this problem is the "controversy over Spanish science" to which Unamuno referred on many occasions, particularly in his writings between 1897 and 1905.

For Ortega y Gasset's attitude toward Unamuno on the question of the "europeanization" of Spain, see my book *Ortega y Gasset: An Outline of His Philosophy* (New Haven, Conn., 1957).

The ideas of Américo Castro to which I have referred in this chapter are to be found throughout that author's writings of the last fifteen years; of primary importance is his *The Structure of Spanish History* (translated by Edmund L. King; Princeton, 1954), of which a new and greatly modified edition is in preparation.

Note to chapter five

I have already referred in the text to various works of Unamuno which are important in this chapter. Here, however, I might also indicate *Ensayos III, IV, V,* and part of *Ensayo II,* the novels *Amor y Pedagogía* and *Niebla,* the short stories in *Tres novelas ejemplares y un prólogo* (especially the "prólogo"), *Cómo se hace una novela,* and *De esto y aquello II.* Also important are the articles collected by Manuel García Blanco under the title "La raza y la lengua" in Volume VI of the *Obras completas,* and the revealing series of articles on style entitled "Alrededor del estilo" in Volume IV of the *Obras completas* (and in *De esto y aquello IV*). See also Unamuno's "Oración inaugural del Curso académico 1934–35," delivered at the University of Salamanca and collected in Volume VII of *Obras completas.* Also there are several important allusions to the "word" as "living word" and as "poetry" in *Del sentimiento trágico de la vida.*

Perhaps more than to any other of his concerns, Unamuno returned again and again to the subject of this chapter. Since he felt he was a "voice" whose mission was to awaken, stimulate, and even irritate his readers in order to lead them into themselves, there is not a single one of Unamuno's writings without some bearing, direct or indirect, on the problem of the nature and function of the "word."

The quotation from Jean Cassou is from his preface to the French edition (1925) of *Cómo se hace una novela.*

The words of Ernst Robert Curtius are from his essay on Unamuno, collected in his *Kritische Essays zur europäischen Literatur* (Bern, 1950).

Note to chapter six

All of Unamuno's novels and short stories are important as background material for this chapter. The most famous of these have been mentioned in the text; the rest are included in the first section of the bibliography. In order to understand how Unamuno understood and created his fictional works, one should at least read *Paz en la guerra, Niebla, Tres novelas ejemplares y un prólogo,* and *San Manuel Bueno, mártir.*

Many of the problems raised by the "fictional character" and his relation to "reality" are intimately related to the problems posed by the nature of man and his relation to God. Therefore, since the nature of man and his relation to God were treated in chapter two, the reader should consult not only those works mentioned in the present note but also those in the note to chapter two. The two plays, *El otro* and *El hermano Juan o el mundo es teatro,* should also be consulted in connection with the present chapter.

The thesis of Julián Marías is advanced in his book *Miguel de Unamuno* (Madrid, 1943) and in the prologue that he wrote to the edition of Unamuno's *Obras Selectas* (Madrid, 1949).

In this chapter I have dealt with the question of a "contemplative" Unamuno—in no way incompatible with our "conflictive" Unamuno—which Carlos Blanco Aguinaga has subsequently made the subject of a book mentioned in the note to chapter one, *ad finem.*

Note to chapter seven

This chapter is an attempt at descriptive ontology based upon language, that is, upon the author's use of language. It may also be taken as an example of description of "the world of an author" —using the term "world" in a sense that I intend to clarify in a future book on the question. Unamuno's entire work ought to be examined to this end, with primary attention being given to those words and expressions which recur most frequently, and to any other words and expressions which constitute variations on, or shadings of, these.

Bibliography

Works of Unamuno

BOOKS PUBLISHED IN UNAMUNO'S LIFETIME:

En torno al casticismo (Madrid, 1895) [later reprinted in *Ensayos I*]
Paz en la guerra (Madrid, 1897)
De la enseñanza superior en España (Madrid, 1899)
Tres ensayos (Madrid, 1900) [includes: "¡Adentro!" "La ideocracia," "La fe," later reprinted in *Ensayos II*]
Amor y pedagogía (Barcelona, 1902)
Paisajes (Salamanca, 1902)
De mi país. Descripciones, relatos y artículos de costumbres (Madrid, 1903)
Vida de Don Quijote y Sancho, según Miguel de Cervantes Saavedra, explicada y comentada (Madrid, 1905; 2d enl. ed., Madrid, 1914)
Poesías (Bilbao, 1907)
Recuerdos de niñez y mocedad (Madrid, 1908)

Mi religión y otros ensayos (Madrid, 1910)

Rosario de sonetos líricos (Madrid, 1911)

Por tierras de Portugal y España (Madrid, 1911)

Soliloquios y conversaciones (Madrid, 1911)

Contra esto y aquello (Madrid, 1912)

El porvenir de España (Madrid, 1942) [Unamuno-Ganivet correspondence previously published in the newspaper, *El Defensor de Granada,* 1897]

Del sentimiento trágico de la vida en los hombres y en los pueblos (Madrid, 1913)

El espejo de la muerte (*Novelas cortas*) (Madrid, 1913)

Niebla (*Nivola*) (Madrid, 1914)

Ensayos, 7 vols., Madrid (Vols. I, II, III, 1916; Vols. IV, V, 1917; Vols. VI, VII, 1918)

Abel Sánchez (*Una historia de pasión*) (Madrid, 1917)

El Cristo de Velázquez. Poema (Madrid, 1920)

Tres novelas ejemplares y un prólogo (Madrid, 1920)

La tía Tula (Madrid, 1921)

Andanzas y visiones españolas (Madrid, 1922)

Rimas de dentro (Valladolid, 1923)

Teresa: rimas de un poeta desconocida (Madrid, 1923)

De Fuerteventura a París. Diario íntimo de confinamiento y destierro vertido en sonetos (Paris, 1925)

Cómo se hace una novela (Buenos Aires, 1927)

Romancero del destierro (Buenos Aires, 1928)

Dos artículos y dos discursos (Madrid, 1930)

La agonía del cristianismo (Madrid, 1931) [French translation, *L'agonie du christianisme,* published in Paris, 1925]

San Manuel Bueno, mártir y tres historias más (Madrid, 1933)

Discurso leído en la soleme apertura del curso académico 1934–1935 en la Universidad de Salamanca (Salamanca, 1934)

Most of the above books have often been reprinted. Unamuno published, besides, hundreds of articles and essays in Spanish and

Spanish-American newspapers and literary magazines. Among his plays, the following may be mentioned: *La Esfinge* (1909), *La Venda* (1913), *Fedra* (1921), *Soledad* (1921), *Raquel* (1921), *El Otro* (1932), *El hermano Juan o El mundo es teatro* (1934).

BOOKS PUBLISHED POSTHUMOUSLY:

La ciudad de Henoc. Comentario 1933 (Mexico, 1941)
Cuenca ibérica (Lenguaje y paisaje) (Mexico, 1943)
Temas argentinos (Buenos Aires, 1943)
La enormidad de España (Mexico, 1944)
Paisajes del alma (Madrid, 1944)
Visiones y comentarios (Buenos Aires, 1949)
De esto y aquello, 4 vols., Buenos Aires (I, 1950; II, 1951; III, 1953; IV, 1954)
Cancionero (Buenos Aires, 1953)
Teatro (Barcelona, 1954)
En el destierro (Recuerdos y esperanzas) (Madrid, 1957)
Inquietudes y meditaciones (Madrid, 1957)
Cincuenta poesías inéditas (1899–1927) (Madrid, 1958)
Mi vida y otros recuerdos personales, 2 vols. (Buenos Aires, 1959)

Most of the above volumes include articles published in book form for the first time.

A collection of so-called complete works (*Obras completas*) is now being published, ed. M. García Blanco, Barcelona, 10 vols., 1950 ff.

English translations

Tragic Sense of Life, trans., J. E. Crawford Flitch, introductory essay by S. de Madariaga. London: Macmillan, 1921; reprinted, New York: Dover Publications, 1954 [a translation of *Del sentimiento trágico de la vida*].

Essays and Soliloquies, trans. J. E. Crawford Flitch. New York: A. A. Knopf, 1925 [a translation of *Soliloquios y conversaciones*].

Life of Don Quixote and Sancho according to Miguel de Cervantes Saavedra expounded with comment by Miguel de Unamuno, trans. Homer P. Earle. New York: A. A. Knopf, 1927 [a translation of *Vida de Don Quijote y Sancho*].

The Agony of Christianity, trans. Pierre Loving. New York: Payson and Clarke, Ltd., 1928. Another translation by Kurt F. Reinhardt, New York: Frederick Ungar Publishing Company, 1960 [a translation of *La agonía del cristianismo*].

Mist. A Tragi-comic Novel, trans. Warren Fite. New York: A. A. Knopf, 1928 [a translation of *Niebla*].

Three Exemplary Novels and a Prologue, trans. Angel Flores. New York: A. and C. Boni, 1930. Reprinted, with introduction by Angel del Río. New York: Grove Press, Inc., 1956 [a translation of *Tres novelas ejemplares y un prólogo*].

Perplexities and Paradoxes, trans. Stuart Gross. New York: Philosophical Library, 1945 [a translation of *Mi religión y otros ensayos,* with minor alterations].

The Christ of Velazquez, trans. Eleanor L. Turnbull. Baltimore: Johns Hopkins Press, 1951 [a translation of *El Cristo de Velázquez*].

Poems, trans. Eleanor L. Turnbull. Foreword by John A. Mackay. Baltimore: Johns Hopkins Press, 1953 [Spanish and English on opposite pages] [a translation of poems from various sources].

Abel Sánchez and Other Stories, trans. Anthony Kerrigan. Chicago: Henry Regnery Company, 1956 [a translation of *Abel Sánchez* and a few additional stories from various books].

A sizable number of essays, articles, and stories from a great variety of Unamuno's books have been translated and published in English and American journals.

Works on Unamuno

Only works and essays related to the topics discussed in the present book are mentioned.

Barja, C., *Libros y autores contemporáneos,* 1935, pp. 39–47.

Torre, Guillermo de, "El rescate de la paradoja" (originally published in 1937) and "Unamuno y Clarín (originally published in 1924), in *La aventura y el orden,* 1943.

Kessel, J., *Die Grundstimmung in M. de Unamunos Lebensphilosophie,* 1937.

Marías, Julián, *Miguel de Unamuno,* 1943.

Oromí, Miguel, *El pensamiento filosófico de M. de Unamuno,* 1943.

Mesnard, P. and R. Ricard, "Aspects nouveaux d'Unamuno," *La vie intellectuelle,* XIV, 2 (1946), 112-139. Also, F. Meyer, "Kierkegaard et Unamuno," *Revue de Littérature comparée,* XXIX (1955), 478–492.

González Caminero, N., *Unamuno. I. Trayectoria de su ideología y de su crisis religiosa,* 1948.

Aranguren, J. L. L., "Sobre el talante religioso de Unamuno," *Arbor,* XI (1948), 485–503.

Benítez, Hernán, *El drama religioso de Unamuno,* 1949.

López-Morillas, J., "Unamuno and Pascal. Notes on the Concept of Agony," *Publications of the Modern Language Association,* XLV (1950), 998–1010.

Serrano Poncela, S., *El pensamiento de Unamuno,* 1951.

Clavería, Carlos, *Temas de Unamuno,* 1953.

Catalán Menéndez-Pidal, Diego, "Aldebarán," *Cuadernos de la Cátedra Miguel de Unamuno,* V (1953).

García Blanco, Manuel, *Don Miguel de Unamuno y sus poesías,* 1954.

Meyer, François, *L'ontologie de M. de Unamuno,* 1955.

Calvetti, C., *La fenomenologia della credenza in M. de Unamuno,* 1955.

Sánchez-Barbudo, A., *Estudios sobre Unamuno y Machado,* 1959.

Blanco Aguinaga, Carlos, *El Unamuno contemplativo,* 1959.

Zubizarreta, Armando F., *Tras las huellas de Unamuno,* 1960.

Articles on Unamuno, complete bibliographical information, and Unamuniana in the series *Cuadernos de la cátedra Miguel de Unamuno,* ed. Manuel García Blanco, 1948 ff.